Cliff...bers
C...TH
...N

Panda 🐼 *Books*

PUBLISHING

ISBN 0 9507775 6 0

CONDITIONS OF SALE

Typeset by T&O Graphics, Oulton Broad, Suffolk
Printed in Great Britain by Richardson Printing Limited, Oulton Broad, Suffolk

Preface

I am not a historian, but having had an interest in photography from an early age, I have been able to record aspects of local history on film for much of this century. So although this volume contains aspects of Great Yarmouth's history and whilst it is historical in the sense that it is a record of things past, my intention is that it should be a reminiscence of the Yarmouth and Gorleston of my lifetime.

The rate of environmental, sociological, economic and habitual change during the twentieth century has been much greater than any other. Great Yarmouth and Gorleston have seen these changes. They have witnessed changes in the habits of holidaymakers. They have seen the herring fishing reach its zenith and fall to its nadir. In travel, the railways have risen and fallen and aviation has much changed since Sir Alan Cobham came to the area in 1929 seeking to popularise air travel by giving trips in his *Youth of Britain* and *Spirit of Youth*. Buildings have changed or been demolished. The South Denes, once an open space, has been covered by industrial development, much of it connected with the new oil and gas industries. In the port the shape and motive power of the ships has changed. So many houses have been built in Gorleston that its population now exceeds that of its neighbour.

Most of these changes have been chronicled in this book. I hope it will give younger readers an idea of the Yarmouth and Gorleston of yesteryear and to those who are older, bring happy memories.

Clifford Temple
September 1984

▲ St. Nicholas Church before it was bombed during World War Two.

Introduction

"Fings ain't wot they used t'be" was a popular song a few years back. These words are especially appropriate when comparing the Yarmouth of a half century ago with the Yarmouth of the present day. For never in the world's history has there been such a rapid transition as that experienced during this period, for we have seen the passing of the steam train, the electric trams, the picturesque sailing and steam-driven ships, the fussy little wooden paddle-wheel tugs and the London excursion steamers. Gone too are the many windmills with their sails revolving in the breeze whilst grinding corn or draining water from the marshes. And one of man's best friends, the horse, is now a rare sight on the roads and often seen only at shows and circuses.

Fashions have obviously undergone great changes. Ladies used to wear cumbersome dresses with petticoats, their long trailing skirts actually sweeping the floor as the wearers walked about. Most of the menfolk wore dark coloured clothing, with highly starched white collars, and all wore hats. Even during the glorious summer months, holiday-makers could be seen wearing their 'Sunday-best' — no shorts or denims for them! — and none would dream of exposing their bodies to the sun's rays unless it was their feet and ankles while paddling in the sea. The ladies even carried parasols to ward off the sun from their lily-white faces.

Compared with today's wages, earnings were very low. To compensate, however, goods were very cheap, coal for instance costing only one shilling per hundredweight and a man's suit, comprising trousers, jacket and waistcoat, cost forty-two shillings and sixpence. Before going further into the joys, sorrows and experiences of that generation, a short potpourri of Yarmouth's history may interest the newcomer to the town and be of help to students and the younger generation.

Great Yarmouth was — and indeed still is — built on a sandbank which thrust its way out of the sea near the beginning of the Christian era. Soon it began to increase in size, and fishermen began to visit it each autumn in search of herrings, which abounded in the adjacent sea at that time of the year. Then in the year 495 Cerdic, a Saxon prince, with Cenric his son, landed there with the crews of his five ships and they plied their trade as fishermen. Cerdic named it 'Cerdic Shore' and built there a fortification to ward off any would-be invader. This Cerdic settlement was neither town nor hamlet, but still the sandbank formed off the coast between two channels of the river Yare. It was between these two havens that the river entered the sea. Eventually the sandbank became firm land, and temporary booths were erected by the fishermen who found it ideal for their trade. The new town quickly increased in population due to an influx of foreigners from Holland, France and Norway, who came each year from Michaelmas to Martinmas for the herring fishing. Eventually in 1008, dwellings were erected on the highest part of the ground, called 'Fuller's Hill', no doubt after the first fisherman to build a house there.

In time Yarmouth became the most flourishing sea port on this part of the English coast and the town acquired a certain degree of importance, so that its inhabitants deemed it necessary to take precautions to provide for its defence in case of sudden invasion. A petition was sent to King Henry III seeking permission to erect a wall around the town, and on 28th September 1262, the King granted the Charter. The project commenced but it turned out to be a bigger undertaking than expected, and took 111 years to complete. One of the reasons for the delay was the terrible 'Black Death' which visited the town in 1349 and carried off 7000 out of a population of 9000. There were hardly sufficient numbers living to bury the dead, let alone erect the fortifications, but by 1396, the work was completed. There were twenty towers, including the four on the North and South Gates, a long semi-circular wall measuring 2280 yards long, 23 feet high and seven feet thick, and ten gates. It was immediately surrounded with a moat across which bridges were thrown at every gate enabling ships laden with produce to land their cargoes at any part of the town. Because the town was confined within these walls, the houses were densely packed together. In order to cross from one side of the town to the other, 145 narrow streets were formed like a grid iron and thus originated the

famous Yarmouth 'Rows'. After many attempts at making a haven, one was finally built by a Dutchman, Joas Johnson, at the end of the sixteenth century, and this is still in use.

With the ever-increasing population, a church was built by a Burgundy priest named Felix in 636. The original church is probably that named St. Bennet's in the Doomsday Book. In 1101, Herbet de Losinga took over the church and renamed it St. Nicholas. Each succeeding reign saw some addition made to the church and in 1250 when Henry III was King, the Bishop of Norwich, Walter de Suffield, erected the building which the present generation knows. It was said that there could not have been a more majestic or imposing parish church in the whole of England. The church had an intriguing feature unknown in other churches — a Whalebone Seat, sometimes called the Devil's Seat. Part of a whale was washed ashore at Caister and brought to Yarmouth where it was deposited in the churchyard and left for 200 years before being placed in a niche in the church for use as a seat. Tradition has it that newly-weds used to rush to sit on it, for the first to do so would 'wear the trousers' for the rest of their married life! Sadly this fine church which claimed to be the largest parish in England fell victim to a fire blitz by German planes during the Second World War, leaving it a roofless empty ruin. Restoration began in 1957 when the ancient walls were renewed. Today, superb stained glass, a fine organ, intricate furnishings and a Norman font make it one of the most splendid churches in England. However, the Whalebone Seat is no longer there as it was carried away with rubble during rebuilding.

Yarmouth has a great naval history and in the 14th century, the naval strength of the port was greater than that of any other in England, including London. In fact in 1337, Yarmouth actually had a navy of its own, comprising twenty men-of-war and called the 'Yarmouth Navy'. Yarmouth was the 'Scapa Flow' for the English fleet and one of the chief gateways to the Continent. Such a conspicuous part was played by Yarmouth throughout the war with France — she sent out 42 ships and 1075 men — that King Edward III granted that the Royal Arms be added to those of the Borough. In 1799, Admiral Duncan took over the fleet anchored in Yarmouth Roads (that is the safe sea passageway between dangerous sandbanks and shore) and on 3rd October sailed from the Roads to defeat the Dutch fleet off Camperdown, returning to Yarmouth with seven of the Dutch ships as prizes. To commemorate this victory, a new terrace of houses near the Wellington Pier were named 'Camperdown'. (Incidentally, it was this Admiral who had earlier captured the famous French frigate *Lutine*, whose bell is now rung at Lloyds of London when an important announcement is to be made.) The *Lutine* was added to the fleet of George III but in 1799, she began her final ill-fated trip from Yarmouth Roads loaded with bullion worth three million pounds and was wrecked.

From the time of Edward III to that of Edward VI, the Admiralty considered Yarmouth opinion of paramount importance as a guide to their designers and later, when Lord Fisher was at the Admiralty, it was the custom to send all the important ships to the Yarmouth Roads so that the local magnates, shipwrights and seamen could pass judgment on their appearance and probable effectiveness. Clearly, the port richly deserves its status as a secondary Cinque Port, as well as its full name of *Great* Yarmouth!

Yarmouth, then, made its name as a seafaring place but today if you ask people what they know of the town they will no doubt say, "It's a seaside resort!" More of this and more about the maritime and fishing aspects in later chapters.

The three cottages in Row 8 which became Yarmouth's first Methodist Chapel. ▶

▲ Row No. 8. One of the few remaining of the original 145. This Row contained three cottages which were once the Methodist Chapel, opened by John Wesley in 1783.
The narrow rows ran from east to west and it is said that the draught so caused kept the town smelling sweet.

The famous 'Troll' cart, made specially in Yarmouth to negotiate the narrow Rows. The shafts were ▶ outside the wheels so that whatever gap the shafts could get through, so could the whole cart.

◄This is how we all like to think of the countryside, although we are never likely to see it so again. It was actually the main road at Caister!

▲One of the imaginative schemes undertaken by the Council in recent years has been the uncovering and preservation of parts of the old town wall, the building of which began in the reign of Henry III and took 130 years to complete. The photo shows the Blackfriars tower. Legend has it that the bricked up portion on the left contains the remains of a soldier and his horse.

◄The last Yarmouth windmill. A drainage mill that worked at Ashtree Farm, Acle New Road until the 1953 gales when the sails were blown off.

▲ The interior of what is now the Elizabethan House Museum as it looked in 1900. It was built in 1596 and it is said that here in 1648 discussions took place concerning the execution of Charles I.

Great Yarmouth — Then and Now

In contrast to present-day guest houses, motels and holiday camps with colour television and other entertainment laid on, holiday-makers at the beginning of the century were quite content to spend a week at a private dwelling-house whose owners would let their spare rooms, and sometimes their own, during the short summer season. Cheap excursion trains used to bring hordes of holiday-makers to the coast, a real task of endurance for some, as many trains had no corridors and mothers with young children were frequently driven to using the children's buckets for a purpose for which they were not intended! The excursion trains were so filthy that one needed a bath on arrival, but sadly most could not have one because few houses had such a facility.

Early in the reign of George V, holiday-makers found Yarmouth an attractive place. It had fine sands for the children to play on, numerous sailing and rowing boats plying from the beach for a 'trip on the briny' and safe bathing, albeit from cumbersome bathing machines, which were box-like structures on four wheels drawn to the water's edge by a horse. Another attraction was the lofty 150 feet high Revolving Tower which, as its name suggests, had a caged platform which revolved as it ascended the tower, enabling people to remain in one place and yet see a complete view of the town, surrounding countryside and even the spire of Norwich Cathedral (more than twenty miles away) on a clear day. Cockle, oyster and whelk stalls stood at intervals along the length of the promenade and at the base of the tower buildings, the smell of their vinegar heavy in the air. Ladies too were seen in their spotless white aprons selling shrimps, while ice-cream vendors and the 'hoky-poky' men with their hand-barrows did a roaring trade.

As today, the Britannia Pier was always well patronised. With its handsome pavilions, domes and turrets, it was quite an event to just sit on the Pier watching the ladies promenading in their long trailing dresses, and carrying parasols to ward off the sun's rays from their lily-white faces. Everyone in those early years seemed to be dressed in their 'Sunday-best', and all wore hats.

Crack regimental bands were engaged to give performances on the Britannia and Wellington Piers, with firework displays each Thursday evening. No-one ever went hungry because Yarmouth sands were simply littered with refreshment stalls selling steaming hot tea at a penny a cup, with cakes, buns, biscuits and ice-cream for the asking. Displayed around the stalls were wood and iron spades, buckets, kites, balls and toy model yachts. Beach concert parties were often held, such as *Chappell's Promenade Concert* and later *The Troubadours*. Punch and Judy Shows always attracted large crowds of children, as indeed they do today. Very popular too was the *Hippodrome* which apart from the usual circus routine had a 'sunken ring' which was flooded with water. Thrilling and spectacular displays in this sunken ring included a show in which 'real redskins' were 'shooting the rapids' in real birch canoes, the 'rapids' being built high up in the 'gods'. With the canoes being driven into the pool beneath, it was thrilling to see the 'redskins' brandishing their tomahawks and shouting wild 'war whoops' as they plunged over the waterfall into the inky waters of the 'lake' below!

'Doodles' was the *Hippodrome's* favourite clown, who always managed to get the crowds roaring with laughter. Another favourite clown was Yarmouth's own 'Whimsical Walker' (the favourite clown of Bertram Mills' Circus), who retired and ended his days owning a shooting gallery on the quayside at Gorleston.

In the late 1920s and early 'thirties, Yarmouth was able to see and enjoy the latest London successes at the *Aquarium*. These included many musical comedies such as *Chu Chin Chow, Lilac Time, No, No Nanette, Mr. Cinders* and many others, all with first class artistes. Later came the craze for 'Big Band' shows so the popular band leaders of radio were engaged to give performances, including Jack Payne and Jack Hylton. Where formerly the town piers had engaged Pierrot and 'Follies' shows, the scene was now changed, presenting radio and television stars. The whole show more or less centred around the main 'star', Ronnie Ronald being one of the first at the Wellington. From that time Yarmouth has seen hundreds of television performers and celebrities, some costing

▲ A picture of Yarmouth beach taken from the Revolving Tower in 1908 and full of interest. Note, particularly, the stalls on the beach and the bathing machines. The dome at the top of the 'Helter Skelter' on Britannia Pier finished up and is still in existence, as a summer house, in the garden of a riverside bungalow at Horning.

The Revolving Tower which stood near the ▶ Britannia Pier. It was dismantled during the Second World War and used for scrap.

thousands of pounds per week — and some not worth a tenth of the money paid for them!

Although vast numbers of holiday-makers travelled to Yarmouth by train each year, many also chose to arrive on one of the famous London paddle-steamers, or 'Belle Boats' as they were called, which due to the very low fares were always teeming with holiday-makers. On fine days the trip by sea from London was very enjoyable, but on less pleasant days, many came ashore looking very green. A local hotelier, Joe Powell, sent horse-drawn cabs to the quayside to pick up his 'lambs', young men who were to spend a week at his Garibaldi Hotel. They were mainly young office clerks bent on having a good time whilst raising money for local charities. Sometimes they took over from the organ grinder, dancing round the barrel organ and collecting money from onlookers at the same time. However, if by chance they saw a courting couple on the sands, they would surround them and sing, to the couple's embarrassment and the spectators' delight, *When we are married* at the tops of their voices! They were famed for their efforts and raised much needed funds for the charities of their choice.

Near Nelson's Jetty, which lies between the two piers, four-horse brakes used to take on passengers for a trip out to the country or the Broads. Perched up high on this conveyance, one could get a wonderful view of the countryside but should it rain, a tarpaulin would be unhitched from a looped frame on the brake, giving the appearance of a covered wagon (which of course it was) in a cowboy movie. Obviously no more sightseeing could be done until the rain ceased. In addition to beach boats, paddle-wheel steamers sailed from the South Quay making for Scroby Sands and the 'bell buoy'. Smaller steamships also took passengers for river trips and to the Broads, some even to Norwich. Most passengers were delighted and amazed to see so many windmills on the river banks as they passed by, their giant sails revolving in the breeze.

A pleasant day could be spent at Gorleston by boarding the 'two-ended' boats at the South Quay, and most enjoyed seeing the endless variety of craft in the river as they went along. These included large steam cargo vessels busy unloading stacks and stacks of timber, coal boats, dredgers, brown-sail barges and even windjammers. The river boats were called 'two-ended' because they never turned round for the return journey, but just went backwards and forwards all the time. One of them, the *Yarmouth*, has been preserved at St. Katharine's Dock in London. Now unknown by many were the 'Johnny Onionmen', dressed in clogs, corduroy trousers and smocks, who came ashore from their sailing craft to sell the long strings of onions which were hanging from long poles carried on their shoulders.

A 'must' for visitors and locals alike was to promenade in the Wellington Gardens. It was a veritable 'monkey parade' where the young men and women could meet and go courting. Various events took place there, including gymkhanas, sports events and Naval Cadet Reviews. The 'Scenic Railway', close by, and the caves, were always a great attraction to the holiday-makers, as were the nanny goats to the young children. Budding ocean yachtsmen could spend the whole of their days sailing their toy yachts in the Nelson Garden yacht pond, without being in the way or in danger. It was a model yacht pond of ample proportions, but is, alas, no more. Half the gardens were made into a large boating lake and the yacht pond was absorbed by this redevelopment which continued, with minor modifications, until recently. Then half the pond was drained and replaced by the spectacular *Alpen Blitz*, the other half remaining as a lake for the rather more sedate 'Whirly' boats.

Mention of the goats reminds me of an occasion during my childhood when my mother took me to feed those endearing animals. At the time we ran a boarding house and as we had a plentiful supply of shelled pea-pods, thought it would be nice to take them to the goats. The goats were harnessed to miniature carriages at the time, but these did not appear to affect the goats' appetites, for the pods were quickly devoured. However, as we began to walk back home, we heard loud shouting, the rumble of wheels and the noise of hooves hitting the road. As we turned round, we were met by the sight of almost a dozen goats tearing along with their carriages, and their owner in hot pursuit, and using language not usually heard in public. Needless to say, there were no more trips to feed the goats.

In recent years, many of Great Yarmouth's former attractions have given way to more modern things. Gone are the steam trains which brought thousands of visitors to Yarmouth each summer, gone are the London steamers and the two sea-trip paddle steamers *United Service* and *King Edward VII*. The ornate pier pavilions, sailing beach boats, four-horse brakes, the Revolving Tower, the beach concert parties and Regimental Band performances have all disappeared. Even the shrimp seller is a rare sight today, although many of the beach stalls can still be seen at their new location on the Promenade. With the changing times, one is tempted to wonder whether people really are as happy and carefree as they used to be in the days when money was scarcer and folk had largely to find their own entertainment.

▲ What a change from today's *Hippodrome* forecourt! In 1909 little girls wore 'pinnies', ladies wore long skirts and everyone wore hats to watch a Punch and Judy Show.

▲ The bandstand in Wellington Gardens eventually gave way to a roller skating rink. In the background can be recognised what is today *The Biergarten*. Originally it was a winter garden purchased from Torquay at the beginning of the century and brought to Yarmouth — not a pane of glass was smashed in transit.

◄ In 1910 you could be entertained by a 'crack' regimental band playing at the Wellington Pier Gardens.

▲
Russ Conway who was appearing at the Wellington Pier.

Yarmouth holiday crowds have always been entertained by the top showbiz stars of the day — some have become almost national institutions, others have sunk without trace. Our pictures show how some of them used to look.

◄Rolf Harris at Gorleston Swimming Pool.

▲Bob Monkhouse at Gorleston.

Billy Fury on the Britannia Pier. ▶

◀ *Chappell's Promenade Concert,* 1909. The concert parties were held on the sands, approximately where the *Marina* stands today. Notice the men's headgear: bowlers, pill-boxes, toppers and caps.

▲ How were you entertained in 1955? By going to the open air *Marina Theatre,* of course. This crowd are packed in to see *Neville Bishop and his Wolves* (who?) and an amateur talent contest.

◀ Yarmouth seems crowded in the summer nowadays. In the 1950's it must have been murder — although when on holiday, with Charlie Chester and The Beverley Sisters to entertain you, what more could you ask?

◀ In the early 1960's the *Sunday Pictorial* arranged 'beauty contests'. They appear to have been very popular!

▲ The fountains, illuminated at night, adjacent to the old *Marina Theatre*, which gave much pleasure to visitors. The bases are still in use as plant holders.

◀ At the old *Marina* — this is how beauty contestants looked in 1953.

◄ The old entrance to the *Pleasure Beach.*

▲ The view looking towards the *Pleasure Beach* and 'Golden Mile' from Nelson's Monument in 1984. Notice how the once open South Denes have been taken over by industry.

◄ Nothing remains the same. The new 'Twentieth Century' entrance to the *Pleasure Beach.*

◄ A solid tyre charabanc on Theatre Plain preparing to take sightseers to the countryside. These vehicles sounded the death knell for the four-horse brakes.

◄ For the children — from about 1908 enjoyment could be had from a ride on a goat cart.

26

◄1947 saw the last of the four-horse brakes working at Yarmouth. You used to be able to go on a sight-seeing trip to the surrounding countryside or Norfolk Broads on one of these.

▲Advertising as it used to be. A well known firm advertising their beef suet in the mid 1920's, in Nelson Road North opposite the old MGN Beach Station.

The mode of transport in 1906 ▶
— the trams working along the seafront.

▲The Fair at the Market Place in 1953.

Yarmouth Market Place at lunch time on a hot summer's day in 1984. The difference, not only ▶ scenically, but in the atmosphere invoked is incredible.

◄King Street in 1907. Although it is midsummer most people are very fully attired. The street was probably busier then that it is today.

▲The Market Place outside Palmer's in 1909. The boards on the cart in the foreground are advertising *The Nigger Minstrels* something which, quite rightly, could not be seen today. Palmer's store was founded in 1837 by Gaywood Burton Palmer and today is still entirely owned by the family.

◄How we went to our graves! A rare photograph taken early this century of a funeral procession.

The Benedictine Priory was founded in Yarmouth in 1273 and the Priory School opened in 1853. It ▶ is now known as St. Nicholas Middle School but when the change of name occurred is not certain — this matter was the subject of inconclusive debate in the *Eastern Evening News* a few years back.

A curious story associated with school concerns the 'Egyptian Princess'. The school had in its custody some sixty five, or so, years ago a mummy, contained in a casket — about which a gentleman learned in these things would, from time to time give lectures. One day at the school a vile smell was noticed. What was it? A dead rat perhaps? Floorboards were ripped up but no rat was found nor any other cause. Eventually it was discovered that the smell emanated from the coffin. No doubt air or damp had got in causing it to rot. So it was decided to bury the mummy in the churchyard but someone observed that according to ancient custom a mummified princess could not be buried during the hours of daylight. Thus it was at midnight the burial party appeared and the remains were laid to rest.

However, that was not the end of the story. A few weeks later the occupants of the vicarage were awakened by a knocking — but nobody was at the door. The same thing happened the next night. Workmen passing through the churchyard heard knocking coming from inside the church. The keys were obtained but when the building was opened nothing was found. Then the vicarage received another visit from the phantom knocker. The police were called and a cordon thrown round the churchyard. Crowds gathered. Again the tapping was heard from within the church and again nothing was found.

Finally, the smell returned to the classroom. Knowing where to look they reopened the casket and the remains of a leg were found. This was buried with the rest of the body — and the tappings stopped!

1918. Mr. Sillis poses with his class ▶ from the Priory Boy's School. C. R. Temple looking about 66 years younger than he does today is on the left of the back row.

◀ The quiet serenity of the courtyard of the Fishermens Hospital built by the Corporation in 1702 for 'decayed' fishermen. On the right of the picture stands "Charity", Gt. Yarmouth's only statue. The ship above the doorway is a three masted lugger known locally as a "Sash-Marry".

▲ *King Edward VII* being used as a passenger vessel for summer visitors in 1909. Of a dozen such tugs which used to grace Yarmouth river, *King Edward VII* was one of the two paddle tugs which towed the convict ship *Success* into Yarmouth Harbour on 27th July 1903.

▲One of the 'Belle' paddle steamers at the beginning of the century. Here safe in Yarmouth after an eleven hour voyage from London. The fare was ten shillings single and seventeen and sixpence return, calling at various seaside resorts on her way.

▲The *Yarmouth*, one of the famous river boats which used to take trippers between Yarmouth and Gorleston. They were known as the 'backwards and forward boats' because they were constructed to obviate the need to turn round. There used to be six of them plying their trade for nearly 70 years, but times change and, alas, they are no more, although one has been preserved at St. Katherine's Dock in London.

◄The Paddle tug *United Service* was the favourite of the Port tugs. At least, she was a tug in the winter — during the summer she took holiday-makers for trips. Built in 1887, she was crushed by a warship during the last war and sank. She was salvaged but only for the breaker's yard. She is seen here during 'windjammer' days towing a German top-sail schooner *Christian Wolderer*.

▲ A scene you will never see again, two of the 'two ended' river steamers moored at Hall Quay (the *Cobholm* and *Yarmouth*). In the foreground is the former Gorleston lifeboat *Louise Stephens* which arrived on station in 1939. Although no longer a lifeboat she can still be seen upstream of the bridge where she is based and used to give river excursions. A striking feature of the photo is that in an area which today is always crowded with traffic there are only six cars to be seen.

'Modern' Yarmouth — the Market Gates development with the new 'bus station. The architecture is ▶ certainly less interesting than that shown in the older photographs and somehow the feeling of 'business' seems to have gone.

37

The Seaside

For more than two hundred years, Great Yarmouth has been drawing summer visitors to sample the delights of its 'salubrious sea breezes' and enjoy the fine promenade, views of what was once known as the German Ocean and shipping, the bath houses and reading rooms with their copies of the London daily papers. However, it was the railways which helped to make the town one of the premier seaside resorts in the British Isles, a status it still enjoys.

It may seem strange to realise that this annual invasion of the coast owes its origin to a doctor who believed that sea water could be a cure for every ailment and that it could be taken both internally and externally. It was thought to be good for asthma, cancer, tuberculosis, deafness and rheumatism. External use involved cold water bathing by both sexes, but as the ladies were not used to revealing more than a limited part of their anatomy, they took to wearing shapeless flannel dresses, tied at the neck but left unfastened at the bottom. With more and more people seeking cures, pamphlets and books were written on the subject of the benefits of the sea. In 1750 Doctor Richard Russell published such a book in English and Latin. He moved to a village called Brighelmstone and through his ideas on the health-giving properties of the sea came the fame and fortune of Brighton, as it is now called. The custom of sea-bathing soon spread and a Quaker named Benjamin Beale had the idea of building a hut on wheels which could be drawn into the water by a horse and afford privacy whilst bathing. Yarmouth obtained some of these machines in 1768 and built further models based on them.

In 1782, Brighton was visited by royalty, in the person of the Duke of Cumberland, and a year later, George, Prince of Wales, tried the waters. The Prince's bathing came to the ears of the King, who was about to review the Fleet, and he also tried the 'new-fangled cure'. Whether by providence or coincidence, the King's health improved, and his sea-side visits for sea-bathing became an annual event! The King and the Prince made the seaside fashionable among all classes of society. Queen Victoria thought she would try it too, but she did not like the brashness of the ornate pavilion which the Prince had had built at Brighton, so she bought Osborne House on the Isle of Wight.

Later, many visits were paid to Yarmouth by King Edward VII who, while still Prince of Wales, stayed at Shadingfield Lodge on Yarmouth's Promenade in the alleged company of the famous Lily Langtry. Many years later, the Duke of York, later to become King George VI, also visited the seaside at Pakefield, and joined in many sing-songs around a camp-fire with the Boys Brigade and some scout troops. In his youth, Prince Philip also enjoyed a trip to Yarmouth which included a turn on the boating lake.

The advent of the railway naturally made a great difference to Britain's watering places. Queen Victoria approved of the railway travel so, following her example, people from all classes flocked to the railway. Many took advantage of cheap rail day-tickets and 'reduced' family tickets to travel from Norwich to Yarmouth for only ninepence return. Places which were inaccessible before were now within reach, and thus the annual trips to the seaside began. The large paddle-wheel excursion steamers joined the bandwagon and brought hordes of holiday-makers from Tower Bridge in London to many east coast resorts, including Yarmouth. Piers and jetties were designed and built by the steamship companies to facilitate the landing and embarking of passengers. Gradually concert halls and ornate pavilions were built on the piers, and prestigious military bands engaged to entertain the visitors. Large hotels and boarding houses, promenades and flower gardens soon made their appearance, and the popularity of the seaside grew and grew. Fun fairs opened and later donkeys and ponies were provided for the children's amusement. Sailing beach boats also appeared in their scores, as did the smaller rowing boat. At Yarmouth, four-horse brakes were introduced to take visitors on short trips to the countryside and the Norfolk Broads. Steam launches and larger vessels made trips to Reedham or further on to Norwich, while at Yarmouth's South Quay, 'two-ended' river boats ferried people to Gorleston and back.

Like most seaside resorts, Yarmouth had its beach concert parties, one being

Chappell's Promenade Concert, and later *The Troubadors*, and these were sited half-way between Britannia Pier and Nelson's Jetty. Yarmouth acquired a bargain when the Corporation bought Torquay's 'Winter Garden' for £1300. Decorated with palms and hanging baskets of flowers and ferns, it made an ideal skating rink. However, skating was not a profitable venture, so it was later converted into a *Biergarten* with Alpine scenery, chairs, tables, coloured umbrellas and Alpine musicians! The Wellington Gardens were also a 'must' for visitor and local resident alike, for they boasted an ornate bandstand with classical 'musical' statues decorating its top, and regimental bands playing excerpts from opera and the popular tunes of the time. At various times, the spacious grounds were also used for gymkhanas and other sports events, open-air meetings and of course band concerts. Firework displays were a regular event which attained a high standard because of competition from the Britannia Pier! Sadly, the coming of World War II brought about a change of attitude in people's hearts. Most no longer wanted a band performance, so part of the Gardens were made into a zoo, the bandstand was demolished and the remaining area became an open roller-skating rink.

Probably Yarmouth's most valuable asset was — and still is — the Britannia Pier, for it made an important contribution to the town's growth as a holiday resort. It has had many ups and downs. The first pier was built in 1856 at a cost of £6,000 and had an eventful history. Within a year, a ship crashed into it, causing great damage, as a result of which the pier had to be shortened by 80 feet. Ten years later another ship, the schooner *Seagull*, cut through the pier again and took away another 100 feet. The pier was then sold and a handsome new one built with a dome and turrets, and a bandstand to add to its attraction. Opened in 1902, this pier grew in popularity, but on 22nd December 1909, the magnificent pavilion was destroyed by fire during a fierce gale. Another pavilion was built, not quite as ornate as the first, and this one was also destroyed by a fire, allegedly started by suffragettes, on 14th April 1914. Once more a new pavilion was built, and this survived the rigours of the First World War, despite bombardment of the town by enemy warships and mines which floated dangerously close by. It afterwards enjoyed many years of service to the public. In 1928 a new ballroom was added, which was enlarged in 1931 and subsequently visited by the Duke and Duchess of York. Once again however, fire was responsible for its destruction on 3rd August 1932.

With the coming of war in 1939, the centre part of the pier was blown up by the military as an anti-invasion measure. After hostilities ceased, the pier was taken over by two well-known figures in the entertainment world, Prince Littler and Tom Arnold; the gap was bridged and the pier enjoyed fresh popularity with visits from stars of radio and television. That demon fire, however, was not satisfied, for on 20th April 1954 it ravaged the whole pier, sweeping through the woodwork like a knife through butter. The new Ocean Ballroom and restaurant, the 1,230 seat Pavilion Theatre, amusements and children's rides were all destroyed. The new eighty-four foot long bar, the offices and the coastguard lookout at the end of the pier were also devastated. A modern pavilion was then built, so very different from the old familiar 'oriental' type that it was nicknamed the 'aeroplane hangar' by the locals.

A favourite haunt of the youngsters was *Barron's Amusements Arcade* which boasted a roundabout, a switchback railway, waxworks, shooting gallery and a chamber of horrors. Another attraction was the phrenologist, Madame Cook, who had a platform on the beach and an uncanny gift for reading one's character. An unusual tent-like structure which used to stand quite near to her was a *camera obscura*, useful for mothers seeking a lost child, for it threw the whole scene of the beach area on to a white screen.

During the 'twenties, the four-horse brakes began to lose popularity as the accepted mode of transport for sightseers and charabancs took their place. All along the 'Golden Mile', drivers parked their charas while they tried to persuade holiday-makers to take a ride into the country. Many were named after famous racehorses such as 'Sansovino' and 'Spion Kop'. Most had solid rubber tyres and a canvas hood for when it rained.

During this same period, the forecourt of the *Hippodrome* was unoccupied, except for a few hoop-la stalls and, for a time, a stall selling sheet music, with a fine tenor singing some of the songs. The songs were mainly composed by Horatio Nichols and included *Shepherd of the Hills* and *Toy Town Major* which at that time were very popular with the public. The space is now occupied by an amusement gallery with one-arm bandit machines. A similar fate has befallen a once-beautiful glass-roofed shopping arcade where holiday-makers could browse, buy gifts or just seek shelter from the rain. Every type of shop was in it, selling everything from gift novelties, cameras and films to tobacco and antiques. Now it is just a noisy enclosure with blaring pop music and slot machines.

In the 1920s, Yarmouth beachmen had a boost when the Scroby sandbank, which had virtually sunk, reared up once more from the sea. In no time terns, wild fowl and seals made it their new home, and many shipwrecks previously concealed by the sea could be seen once again. The boatmen were quick to seize the opportunity to take holiday-makers out to the 'island' to "see the wrecks and gather birds' eggs" — the latter, of course, was eventually forbidden — and boatloads of people went out to explore, coming away with pockets full of eggs. On one occasion the beach sailing boat *Cambria* went out and landed a party of thirty to forty people on the sandbank. When they tried to leave the island, however, they found that the boat had stuck fast in the sand. Every available motor-boat was summoned to the stuck vessel and a tug-of-war commenced between the score or so of motor-boats pulling at ropes attached to the *Cambria* and the Scroby sandbank. With the help of a rising tide, the motor-boats eventually won and the *Cambria* returned to shore.

It was a vessel built on similar lines to the *Cambria* which on 1st September 1903 suffered one of the worst marine disasters Great Yarmouth had ever known. Three ships of His Majesty's Royal Navy were anchored in the Roads, dressed rainbow-fashion with flags and bunting, and sailing boats and flag-trimmed excursion steamer were busy taking holiday-makers out "to see the fleet". On that day, a beach sailing boat, the *New Skylark*, left the beach just south of the Britannia Pier. Being lunchtime she was only able to secure eight passengers, but her crew consisted of three men plus two musicians, making a total of thirteen people altogether. The sea was like the proverbial millpond and the weather clear. All were enjoying the trip when, rounding the 'bell-buoy' for the trip home, disaster struck. A steamship, the *F. E. Webb*, was approaching at a fast rate and she came straight on, her sharp steel stem cutting into the port quarter of the sailing vessel which filled with water, capsized and sank. At that time, boats did not carry lifebelts or other lifesaving equipment and there was very little wreckage to cling to. The steamship lowered a boat and saved one survivor and Lowestoft fishing trawlers passing by came to the rescue too. In all, seven of the thirteen were saved but all the boatmen were drowned, making it a major tragedy.

Two amusing incidents occurred at Yarmouth during these early years, one in connection with a bathing machine, the other involving the Revolving Tower. According to the state of the tide, bathing machines were towed to the water's edge by horse or further up the beach during an incoming tide. On this occasion the tide was coming in so without further thought, the machine attendant tethered his horse and began pulling the machine to a safer spot further up the beach. Unknown to him, however, the machine had an occupant, a young lady, and the sudden movement of the machine threw her against the door, which opened, leaving her in a sprawling heap on the sand, stark naked. Picking herself up, she ran after the disappearing machine, shouting for the attendant, much to the delight and amusement of spectators watching the scene. The other incident, involving the Revolving Tower, occurred when the cage got stuck at the top, which happened regularly, entailing a long wait for passengers while repairs were carried out to free it. On this occasion a middle-aged lady said that she had an important train to catch and that she would descend by the emergency ladder provided a man came up from below to hold her skirts down, so that onlookers could not gaze at the red pantaloons she was wearing. She descended the ladder amid cheers of scores of holiday-makers, with the man still holding her long skirt and petticoats.

Before the swimming pool was built on Yarmouth's seafront, there used to be a coastguard lookout nearby, comprising a hut with a very tall flagpole and a circular enclosure which kept visitors from prying too close. It was quite a novelty for holiday-makers to see the coastguard come out with a huge telescope, peer at a ship passing through the Roads and then see him getting out an assortment of flags and running them up the flagpole to send a message to the vessel out at sea. All this was necessary because there was no ship to shore telephone or radio in those days. When the swimming pool was completed, the coastguard lookout was shifted to its entrance until, with the passing of time, it too disappeared.

During the 'twenties, to help relieve the dreadful unemployment problem, Yarmouth's Waterways were built. They made a pleasant change from the more boisterous southern end of the resort. In 1937 great alterations and improvements were made to Yarmouth's Central Parade, and the Marina open-air amphitheatre came into being, as well as the illuminated water fountains.

It was said that the Marina was so-named to commemorate the marriage of the Duke of Kent to Princess Marina. At the time of its presentation it was hailed as a god-send to Yarmouth for it was ideal for holding conferences, meetings, band concerts and concert parties. Many people have nostalgic memories of 'Neville Bishop and His Wolves', especially at his entrance holding a mop aloft and leading his band playing *Macnamara's Band* as they walked crocodile fashion among the audience. Sadly, times have changed and in spite of many beauty competitions being held there, All-in Wrestling staged and band concerts given, it finally became a showground for a 'Wild West Saga' with a 'real' sheriff, jail, cowboys on horses, shooting affrays and an exhibition of Golden West memorabilia. It eventually closed to make way for a huge sports centre, also named the *Marina*.

Further north, the fun fair became an Amusement Park and the once-picturesque *Scenic Railway* with 'snow-capped mountains', chalets and caves became the *Roller Coaster*, along with showboats, water chutes, space-ships, Cresta Run and children's trains. 'Clock golf' can be played in the adjacent park which formerly had fine bowling greens and attractively laid-out gardens. The once popular Wellington Gardens, which attracted thousands of people for its band concerts, have seen many changes too. After being divided into two, they became a roller skating rink and a zoo, then were altered to make a model village. Then, not so long ago, they became a centre for devotees of cricket, a huge scoreboard was erected and deckchairs comfortably laid out on the lawn, in semi-circular formation, for the benefit of the enthusiasts. Lolling in comfort, listening to the band and watching the scores was the enviable lot of those with the leisure time available to enjoy their favourite sport.

A subject worthy of note in this chapter is the history of the bathing costume. In the earliest days, there was nude bathing by both sexes. Then followed the wearing of flannel gowns tied at the neck. Then the bodice-pantaloon and frilled bonnet for the ladies, with men wearing what can only be called 'long johns'. Next came the elaborate costumes — not for bathing in but for show — of continental origin with cross-lacing up the legs. The 1920s saw the introduction of the one-piece for both sexes and with it came the 'Mackintosh' era. People objected to paying a fee for just undressing in a machine or tent, so donned their bathing costumes at their hotel or boarding house and, just wearing a 'mac', made for the sea. Having had their bathe, they returned to the hotel either with or without their costume under the mac! The year 1930 saw the first backless costume, which in turn was replaced ten years later by the two-piece suit. By then it was advocated that the sun was beneficial to the body, and therefore it was only logical to expose as much of the body as possible, but keeping within the bounds of public decency. So, the costumes became smaller and smaller until in 1949, the famous 'bikini' costume arrived in Britain from the United States. The 1980s have, of course, seen the return of nude bathing in certain designated areas such as nearby Corton.

As mentioned in another chapter, Yarmouth has always had close links with the Navy and even in the fourteenth century, Yarmouth's naval strength was greater than that of any other English port. When in 1903 the battleships *H.M.S. Majestic, Mars, Jupiter, Prince George, Hannibal, Sutles, Doris, Prometheus* and *Magnificent* were launched, they were sent to Yarmouth Roads where they were lined up off the jetty. On the 3rd October 1903, a throng of sightseers lined the seafront while beachmen did a thriving trade by taking visitors round the fleet. At the end of the First World War, Yarmouth was visited by the 'cream of the Navy', battleships known as the "four Rs", namely *H.M.S. Resolution, Ramilles, Revenge* and *Royal Oak (H.M.S. Royal Oak* was the first warship to be sunk by the enemy in World War II.) All were anchored off the Britannia Pier and one could go on board and peer at the huge guns, go into the gun turrets and down into the ammunition locker and view the enormous shells that the guns would fire. Later Yarmouth was visited by *H.M.S. Warspsite* (of Narvik fame) and *H.M.S. Repulse*, which was probably the largest and longest vessel Yarmouth has ever seen. She too was sunk, by the Japanese in the last world war. However, the vessel which attracted more crowds than any other was the aircraft carrier *Furious*. Not only did visitors queue to go on board, but half a dozen queues formed, stretching from Parade to sea shore.

Other battleships and destroyers to visit Yarmouth included *H.M.S. Norfolk*, which played a prominent part in the sinking of the *Bismarck*, as well as being the first British Navy ship to hit the German raider *Scharnhorst*. Then came the destroyers *Solebay, Saintes, Troubridge* and *Defender*. Yarmouth's namesake, *H.M.S. Yarmouth* has paid a number of visits over the years and even saw service in the South Atlantic in the battle for the Falklands, towing the ill-fated *Sheffield* for as long as was possible. The then new *H.M.S. Norfolk*, a successor to the warship which had been instrumental in the *Bismarck's* demise, visited Yarmouth in the early seventies, looking very different from her former namesake. She was built at the Swann Hunter Group shipyard at a cost of £20 million and launched by the Duchess of Norfolk in November 1967. When she was finally handed over to the Royal Navy three years later, she had Seaslug guided missiles, fired from twin launchers aft, to deal with very fast high-flying aircraft, and Seacat guided missiles for close-range anti-aircraft defence, with four radar-controlled 4.5 in. semi-automatic guns mounted in twin turrets for self-defence and shore bombardment. Missing were the large guns and turrets of the former *Norfolk*, and she did not have the three tall funnels so noticeable in the 'County' class cruisers. The new *Norfolk* was also a destroyer with a crew of 450 and said at the time of her initiation to be "the most modern vessel in the world and a truly fearsome ship of war".

Some years back, the author was reclining in a beach chair near the water's edge at Yarmouth when, in the distance parallel to Scroby Sands, half a dozen destroyers came into view, throwing up quite a picturesque bow wave. Everyone stood up to watch the unusual occurrence, then settled down once more after they had gone from view. But . . . half an hour later there was pandemonium, with half the beach flooded, chairs and rowing boats carried away, chair-sitters drenched and children swept into the sea, as the wash from the destroyers hit the beach! As a result, passing warships were ordered to reduce speed when passing seaside resorts.

Nowadays there is perhaps less danger to the public from passing warships than from passing oil-rig tenders. Not so many years ago, Yarmouth-based passenger ferries left the quayside for day-trips to the Continent. However, as a change and in order to keep up to date, they were persuaded to give visitors the opportunity of a trip out to view the oil and gas rigs, which were becoming quite a common sight just a few miles off the east coast. At close quarters, they are veritable 'towns' on huge stilts towering many feet higher than the visiting vessel.

Many will remember the 1950's style of bathing suit for youngsters. Most will not remember how they were attired for the seaside in 1908.

▲ The ornate pavilion of the Britannia Pier, built by Boulton & Paul of Norwich in 1902 and totally destroyed by fire in 1909.

The original entrance to Britannia Pier — not quite so colourful as the present one! ▶

▲ Not quite so ornate was the second pavilion built to replace the one burned down in 1909. This one was also destroyed by fire, allegedly started by suffragettes, in 1914.

◄ Thirty years ago. The *Scenic Railway* when it *was* 'scenic'.

▲ The fore-runner of those giant multi-coloured slides they have nowadays — Jack and Jill, an attraction at the pleasure beach some 40 odd years ago. Note also, in the foreground, the carriages of the train which used to travel round the perimeter.

◄ Entertainment — 1984 style. The *Alpen Blitz*.

◄ *The Marina* amphitheatre.

Do you remember the old coastguard signal- ►
ling station which stood, surrounded by a wire
fence, for many years on the beach opposite
the Sailors Home? Eventually it was
enveloped by the Bathing Pool and later
ceased operation, its reason for being ceasing
as ships became equipped with radio.

◄ This *was* modern Yarmouth but the swimming pool has been replaced by the new *Marina*
complex.

The interior of the *Winter Gardens* (now the ►
Biergarten) in 1934.

49

▲Bathing huts — on wheels so that they could be towed into the water — on the beach in 1909. At this time most bathers would wear long garments extending from the throat to the ankles and the 'fair sex', as they were known then, would hold on to a rope to prevent themselves from being swept away by the current.

◄If you were an Edwardian and wanted to 'take a trip on the briny' this is how you would take it. The boat is a yawl which has been re-rigged cutter style for convenience of handling.

Grandma enjoying the sands at Yarmouth▶ complete with tippet and hat. Note the bathing-machines in the background.

◄Do you remember the 'sand artist' who used to entertain the holiday crowds with his skill. In 1953 a popular subject was the murderer John Christie.

◄The crowds thronged to the beach on August Bank Holiday in 1909. How uncomfortable they must have been in all those clothes! Note the yawls giving sea trips and the bathing machines available for the few souls who took to the water. The horse on the right of the picture was used to tow the machines to the water.

▼1953. The beach is still popular but the crowds did not wear quite so much in the way of clothing as their Edwardian forebears.

◄The beach on a very hot day at the end of July 1984. People now bring a fence to protect their bit of beach and bathing machines have disappeared along with modesty and the beach stalls. The most striking difference between this and the Edwardian photo is how comparatively few people are using the beach nowadays.

Yarmouth at War

Despite rumours of war, people celebrating the August Bank Holiday in 1914 were as numerous as ever and the Britannia and Wellington Piers were crowded. Sailing and rowing boats took trippers to the 'bell buoy' and back, while the beach concert party prospered. But fears of war were present in people's minds and soon it became a grim reality. All round the coast fishermen who knew the home waters intimately became invaluable in helping the minesweepers. A few Yarmouth and Lowestoft skippers and crew of these craft are still with us. Yarmouth harbour and river were the scene of great activity, being a base for submarines, as well as for the old monitor *Lord Roberts* with its huge gun and the submarine depot ship *Alecto*. The South Denes were used as a base for sea planes of the Royal Naval Air Force. The town also saw the 'blimps', small airships from Pulham in Norfolk known as the 'Pulham Pigs'. On the 19th January 1915 Yarmouth was one of the first towns to be bombed from the air by German Zeppelins and on the 25th April 1916, it was one of the first to suffer bombardment from the sea by enemy ships.

The first attempted sea bombardment took place on the 3rd November 1914, but owing to buoys being moved on Admiralty orders none of the shells reached the shore. The second sea bombardment happened on the author's birthday — 25th April 1916 — of all days! On that day the inhabitants of Yarmouth were awoken by the sounds of gunfire, the rattling of windows and the then unfamiliar shriek of shells passing overhead. Suddenly there was the sound of running feet and soldiers rushing from their billets, whistles blowing, and the sound of the straps of the soldiers' rifles as they passed. The bombardment continued, shells still passing over the houses as bewildered civilians tried to discover what was happening. Suddenly officers arrived and ordered everyone to pack what belongings they could carry and hasten to the Acle New Road and once there to make for Norwich, as the Germans were landing on the beach! However, the rumour proved wrong and the order was rescinded, much to everyone's relief.

The bombardment eventually ceased and it seemed as if with one accord the population of Yarmouth had the idea of making for the promenade and beaches to see what damage had been done and to view the possible craters. Perversely, many were actually disappointed because very little damage could be seen. They had expected hotels and boarding houses to be razed to the ground and vast damage done to the promenade. Rumour had it that the huge aeroplane hangars on the South Denes had been hit, so many made for that site, but the only damage seen was to a few sheds used for the curing of herring on Salmon Road. Early souvenir hunters had already arrived and were picking up and selling pieces of shrapnel and shell splinters, mostly about the size of one's hand. Returning home however, it was reported that the neighbouring town of Lowestoft had suffered much more from the bombardment and sustained many casualties and destruction of homes and other property, with which we commiserated.

One evening in 1915 the author was attracted outside by a strange noise. A traction engine? No! Instead, immediately above the house was an object resembling a huge cigar, its engine throbbing away and instantly recognisable as one of the dreaded Zeppelins. It turned out to be this one that was dropping bombs on the town and which, it was stated, had followed the train in to the Beach Station before continuing southwards along Nelson Road. The bombs damaged houses and a warehouse, killing two people living near St. Peters Road, caused craters in the street and damaged stained glass windows in the nearby St. Peters Church (now the Greek Orthodox Church). What an outcry there was afterwards — "Brutal Murderers" — "Fiendish Behaviour of the Hun" — "Innocent civilians and children" — the papers were loud in their condemnation of this, the very first experience of an English town being bombed from the air. A soldier passing by received a splinter of shrapnel from a bomb and was taken to hospital where a doctor performed an operation to remove the fragment. The doctor later had it cut and polished and made into a tie-pin and ever afterwards claimed that he was the first doctor to attend a casualty through enemy bombing from the air in Britain. Never before had a town suffered such a frightening experience. A substantial money award was made to the dependants of the two who were killed.

There are many schoolboy reminiscences concerning this war that are worth repeating. On one occasion when the air-raid siren sounded, the boys of one school were herded together by their teacher into the nearby St. Nicholas Church, via the school's back entrance. Inside the boys were told to crouch down under the cumbersome wooden pews as a safety precaution against bomb fragments or falling masonry. Needless to say, even in the solemn atmosphere of this ancient church, pranks were played and many a boy's anatomy attacked by a deftly wielded pin from a would-be humourist. During playtime the boys often watched cloud-bursts of shells exploding from Army guns practising on the beaches and elsewhere. The watching of raw recruits being put through their paces on the Marine Parade provided hours of amusement, as did the fraternising with soldiers in the dug-outs and trenches around the Britannia Pier gardens. Boys were even shown how to lob practice hand-grenades over the barbed wire entanglements on the beach. When the Welsh Fusiliers were stationed nearby, they allowed the author and some friends to take out their pet goat — the Regimental Mascot — for exercise. Being rather proud of this privilege, they took it round to show the author's mother. The animal made its way indoors and before it could be stopped, had devoured all the antimaccassars from the chairs and settee, part of the plush table cloth and even some of the plants on the window sill!

One thing that boys all over Britain can thank Yarmouth for is the introduction of the paper aeroplane. Formerly boys were content to fold a piece of paper and make it into a kind of 'triangular dart' which, when thrown, would glide through the air. When the Germans invaded Belgium, the resulting refugees made their way to Yarmouth and the boys attended the Catholic School of St. Mary, off Regent Road. In spite of language barriers, the Yarmouth and Belgian boys soon got on together, and in no time the Belgians were showing the local lads how to fold a piece of paper to resemble a monoplane with wings, body and tail. The Belgians called them *Taubes* after the German planes which had bombed their homes and these paper *Taubes* were certainly a big improvement on the old-type darts and could be made to 'loop the loop' and glide for quite long distances.

Following the Zeppelin raid on Yarmouth, a mid-week prayer meeting was held in the Baptist Church and among the hymns was the line "Singing to welcome the Pilgrims of the Night". It was decided not to sing the hymn again until hostilities had ceased! In contrast, another incident designed to entertain the several thousand troops stationed in the town was a Gymkhana held at the Wellesley Recreation Ground. Amongst the numerous items on the programme was a 'bombing the car' episode which proved both thrilling and amusing. An 'open' car raced round the cinder track and was 'chased' by a bi-plane, flying very low. It was loaded with small bags of flour which were thrown from the plane at the occupants of the car, who soon resembled snowmen! This was followed by a bombardment of soot-bags and a glorious study of black and white resulted.

Another aspect of the War were the speed tests which were carried out at Yarmouth involving planes flying low over the water between the Britannia and Wellington piers. A green volley light was fired when the plane passed the Wellington Pier and red one fired when it passed the Britannia Pier. The then incredible speed of 85 miles per hour was recorded and it is amusing to recall in this supersonic age that the older generation of beach-men who were watching said they "did not believe it, because no man could live at such a speed!"

Peace came in 1918 and life got back to normal but when Neville Chamberlain announced on 3rd September 1939 that Britain was (again) at war with Germany, most people were not surprised. Air Raid Precautions had been in existence for some time, and trenches had been dug and reinforced with sandbags. Gas masks had been issued with smaller child respirators for the two-to-four year olds. Everyone had to carry a mask about with them wherever they went, initially in a simple cardboard box tied with string until more satisfactory holders were provided. Children were evacuated from London to Norfolk, as it was thought that the East Coast would be safe for them and on one weekend, five train loads arrived at Norwich on the Saturday, and a further seven on the Sunday. The former London paddle-wheel pleasure steamers were also mobilised to take thousands of Thames Estuary towns' children to the coast. As the General Steam Navigation Company's ships were assembled, and the evacuee youngsters taken on board, mixed feelings of excitement and fear at leaving parents were experienced by the children. The steamers conveyed children to Yarmouth, Lowestoft and Felixstowe and brought a total of 19,978 youngsters without mishap. However, the 'safe' East Coast proved to be just as unsafe as London, so after a short stay at the seaside, which some had never seen before, the evacuees were moved again — further inland to avoid the many air-raids. Many Yarmouth children were also evacuated and sent to Retford, a market town near the Yorkshire border.

The pleasure steamers were later taken over by the Admiralty and converted into minesweepers and hospital ships, while some played an invaluable part in the Dunkirk evacuation. As in World War I, Yarmouth beach was mined and barbed wire entanglements erected along the length of the shore. The centre of the Britannia Pier was blown up by the military as a counter-invasion measure, and just a few planks of wood spanned the gap for the benefit of the coastguard lookout at the end of the pier.

The town's first real experience of the war came with the air raids. A series of concentrated raids on Yarmouth over the ten day period from 8th to 18th April 1941 resulted in widespread havoc and the deaths of 54 people. A further 119 were injured in the course of 176 attacks on the town between 11th July 1940 and 1st June 1944. In a further 43 raids, bombs fell into the sea, but throughout that long period of attack, the ten days in April 1941 will always be regarded as the worst. For four successive nights in that Easter week, the town was attacked, and after a lull at the weekend, the raiders returned on three consecutive nights. Parachute mines did considerable damage, while the town was lit up with flares dropped by the bombers. It was Yarmouth's first experience of such an attack and resulted in many casualties. While the raid was at its height, two other mines fell at the south end of the town, one in the very congested area of Middlegate Street and the other at the junction of Blackfriars Road and Queens Road. These mines were responsible for the bulk of the casualties — eighteen killed and sixty-eight injured — but it was the incendiary bomb attack which caused the greatest damage to property. It was estimated that four thousand incendiary bombs were rained on the town and its centre soon became a fearful sight as it became enveloped in flames. It was soon realised that the Fire Service would be unable to deal with the sixty-five major fires and two hundred other fires alone and reinforcements were sent into the town from Norwich, Lowestoft, Beccles and Cromer. The Tolhouse and the Science School on the South Quay were damaged in this fire blitz, as were Johnson's Factory in Middlegate Street, the Mission to Seamen Institute, the British Sailors' Society, Education Committee Offices, several shops and Jarrold's Printing Works. Many more raids followed but Yarmouth stood up well to the ordeal.

Warehouses and ships in the harbour were also bombed, and Trinity House suffered a great blow when their tender *Reculver* provided an easy target for a German pilot, while it was out on a peaceful mission of relieving lightship crews off the East Coast. On 20th January 1940, a Dornier bomber dived without warning to attack the defenceless vessel, scored a direct hit at the second attempt, killing an officer and throwing injured men in all directions, and hurling the ship's lifeboats into the sea. There were forty men on board and as the unharmed members of the crew prepared to drag the injured to safety, the Dornier returned to rake the deck with machine gun fire. There was no respite as the German continued the attack for half an hour, scoring four more direct hits with bombs. At the end of it all, there were nearly thirty seamen injured, some of them seriously, and the deck was in a shambles. A trawler came to the rescue and took sixteen of the most badly injured to Yarmouth, while another eight were taken ashore by the Gorleston lifeboat. The last six injured men were rescued by another vessel and all were rushed to hospital. Miraculously the stricken *Reculver* kept afloat and was eventually repaired, but she finally sank when she hit a mine in the Humber later in the same year.

Another memorable but tragic attack was the bombing of the *East Dudgeon Lightship*. The men in the lightships around the coast were used to seeing planes passing overhead, the pilots sometimes waving to them, so they were not unduly alarmed on this occasion when they saw enemy planes coming in their direction. However, this time it was different for the enemy planes swooped to attack, spraying the vessel with machine gun bullets, which shattered the lantern and blasted holes in the cabin. Then they rained bombs on the defenceless vessel, the last scoring a direct hit which left the vessel badly damaged. During the attack the master and crew took to the ship's lifeboat but the planes then disappeared, and the men returned to their vessel which, though damaged, was still afloat. They were more than glad to be back because the weather was so bad, with heavy falls of snow. However, the planes returned to further damage their victim. As the lightship was on the point of sinking, the crew took to the lifeboat again and decided to row to the shore. The wind and heavy seas made rowing hard work and the icy weather slowly numbed them. As dawn broke, the coast was sighted and with hardly any strength left, they rowed towards the beach. Unfortunately a bank of sand was between them and safety, and the boat capsized on the sandbank, throwing them all into the sea. Somehow, in spite of the freezing cold, the men managed to reach the shore on their hands and knees, led by a man named John Sanders. He encouraged his mates to follow him but they were too weak to do so and lay at the water's edge. At last John Sanders found a house but it was unoccupied. However, he found a pile a blankets in a nearby shed in which he wrapped himself, undoubtedly saving his life, and then went to sleep. He was found there next morning and taken to his home in Northgate Street to recover from his ordeal. However, a search for his fellow mariners found them dotted about the shoreline in huddled heaps . . . dead from exposure and exhaustion. John Sanders was the sole survivor of the tragic and terrifying Nazi attack.

As in the First World War, Yarmouth was the base for the 'little ships' running out to 'E-Boat Alley' and had that useful commodity for repairing disabled ships in the river, a floating dock, whose services were thankfully used on many occasions. Many unfortunate vessels that had been dive-bombed, strafed with machine-gun bullets, or damaged by mines, were glad of this haven of refuge but two in particular come readily to mind. These were the *Kirnwood* and the *Cree*, the former being one of the longest vessels ever to come into Great Yarmouth harbour. When out in 'E-Boat Alley', the *Kirnwood* had been bombed, set on fire and abandoned by her crew. Captain Sam Spilling then went out in the Yarmouth tug *Richard Lee Barber* and played water on to the disabled and burning ship from the tug's fire gun. When the fire had largely been extinguished, the tug's crew boarded her and with extra hoses completed the task. The tug *Norman* then helped to tow her to Yarmouth Roads where the Yarmouth Fire Brigade spent a further two or three days putting out fires in the engine room and bunkers. The *Kirnwood* was finally brought safely into Yarmouth Harbour and berthed at Bollard's Quay where the Yarmouth Brigade pumped her dry. She was temporarily repaired and towed out of harbour to be a useful member of the defence fleet again. The *Cree* had suffered much the same as the *Kirnwood*, but her steering had gone and she was well down at the stern. Blazing furiously, she had three tugs pumping water on her, but she was in a very bad way. However, the fire was put out, the ship patched up and like the *Kirnwood*, the *Cree* returned to active service after more permanent repairs.

The five years and eight months of the Second World War brought Yarmouth into closer touch with the harsh realities of war than ever before in its long and eventful history. Although the town had suffered attacks from the sea and air during the First World War, the casualties and damage had been slight. Now, however, the frequency of the raids both by day and night was a severe test on the public's morale. From the very first raid, which occurred in the early morning of 11th July 1940 to the last, which was during the night of 1st June 1944, the weird banshee wailing of the siren was heard 2046 times. A total of 10,160 bombs fell on the town, ranging from parachute mines to incendiaries and these killed 217 people and injured 588 more. Among the most tragic incidents were the heavy loss of life of WRNS and ATS girls, when their billets on Queens Road and North Drive were hit in 1943. As always, the main victim of the bombings was property — 1836 houses, shops and commercial premises were destroyed, 1868 seriously damaged and 19,840 slightly damaged. The ancient church of St. Nicholas was reduced to a blackened shell by fire in an incendiary raid on the night of 24th June 1942. St. Peter's Church, which had itself suffered damage in a Zeppelin attack in the First World War, took over as Yarmouth's parish church. Yarmouth also saw 'flying bombs' passing over the town, but the only rocket to land was in a field near Hopton.

Tuesday 8th May 1945 was Victory in Europe Day and Yarmouth experienced a great feeling of relief, but it was not until VJ Day on 15th August that the town felt able to celebrate to the full. However, although the war was over, goods were still rationed, sweet rationing continuing until 1954. Thus it was a godsend when a ship laden with oranges ran aground on the Haisboro' Sands in December 1948. Many crates of oranges had to be dumped overboard to lighten the vessel and enable it to be towed clear of the sand. Soon the beach was overrun with crates of oranges, thousands of loose ones bobbing up and down in the sea. News soon spread and people were quick to seize such an opportunity for worthwhile beachcombing. Customs officers naturally laid claim to the jettisoned fruit, but nevertheless many a household boasted a large bowl of oranges on the sideboard that Christmas!

▼ Preparation for war. The Fourth Norfolk Regiment drilling at Yarmouth in 1914.

▲One of the Zeppelins which flew over Yarmouth and dropped bombs on York Road, St. Peter's Plain and St. Peter's Church on 19th January 1915, killing two people. Its overall length was nearly 600 feet and diameter 40 feet. The airship carried a crew of 40.

▲Damage caused in St. Peter's Plain following the Zeppelin raid on 19th January 1915.

▲ At the beginning of the War children were evacuated from London to places like Yarmouth where it was thought they would be safer. It was not to be and these youngsters have boarded a 'pleasure' steamer and are leaving the port, ultimately, for an inland destination.

▲One of the great boons to vessels needing repairs during the war was this floating dock.

◄The Trinity tender *Reculver.* It was this unarmed vessel that was bombed and strafed by a German Dornier, injuring thirty of her crew of forty.

▲Britannia Pier. The centre was blown up during World War Two as an anti-invasion measure. A baby suspension bridge has been erected to enable the lookout to get to his station at the end of the pier.

▲ The fishing fleet went to war too. This Yarmouth drifter has had her deck strengthened to support a gun and an observation platform built above the wheelhouse. With the appropriate equipment installed she is ready for service as a minesweeper during the First World War.

▼ The Second World War saw the fishing fleet again pressed into service. This time it is a trawler that has been fitted out for use as a minesweeper.

▲Italian prisoners of war taking a break during the unloading of timber during World War Two.

▼All that remained of the shelters adjoining the Nelson Gardens, after Hitler had had a go at the resort.

◄ The aftermath of war. Buildings in the famous 'Row' area after the Second World War.

▲ All that remained of St. Nicholas' — the largest Parish Church in England — after the bombing of June 1942.

◄ The South Quay as it looked from the bridge of a ship during the post-War rebuilding of the town.

Maritime Yarmouth

Great Yarmouth has been very fortunate in recent years, having had two separate visits from the 'Tall Ships', prior to their departure for the Sail Training Association's Tall Ships Race. Their very presence stirred the memories of the older generation recalling the days of their youth when tall stately ships were quite a common sight, entering and leaving harbour and moored at the quayside. They would unload cargoes from the four corners of the earth, their masts towering high above the roofs of the warehouses and wharves. Recalling those far-off days, when the Yarmouth river was a veritable 'forest of masts', collier brigs could be seen discharging coal on the South Quay for the local coal merchants, while barques and barquentines discharged their loads of timber on both sides of the river. Gangs of men could be seen walking precariously along planks of wood from the vessel to the quayside, carrying long lengths of swaying timber on leather 'saddles' attached to their shoulders. Flags of all nations flew from these craft and it was a joy to walk on a Sunday evening to view these ships, and to admire the wonderful carved figureheads at the bows. They were masterpieces in themselves and mostly took the form of a half-clothed female. What a picture these old windjammers made as they were towed into harbour by a fussy little paddle-wheel tug, *United Service*, their sails neatly furled and flying their national flag. Some even carried a picturesque windmill, which was used for pumping bilge water.

Many names come to mind, as perhaps, will the names of oil-rig tenders in the years to come. Possibly the 'tall ship' which created the most interest was the convict ship *Success* when she paid the town a visit. She had come straight from Botany Bay, Australia, and was a floating museum with her prison comprising dark evil-looking cells, whipping posts, chains and leg irons. To make the scene more realistic, fake convicts and guards had been moulded in wax and dressed in appropriate clothing. The Finn barquentine *Estonia* was a frequent visitor to Yarmouth and had been given the name of 'Murder Ship' because of a stabbing incident which happened on board. Another old timer of the mid 1920s was the wooden Finn barque with the most unromantic name of *Fred*, and which carried a windmill. The *Fred* was eventually stranded and became a wreck in 1933. The *Carmen* was yet another wood-built vessel which had the misfortune to become stranded on the beach at Wells, on her maiden voyage. However she was saved by shedding some of her cargo and got off, and made many more visits to Yarmouth afterwards.

Some of the older townsfolk will no doubt recall the occasion in 1926 when a film unit decided to make Yarmouth its location for filming a sea drama. A sailing barque, the *Shakespeare*, was chartered and towed up river to the fishwharf. The public were allowed on board to see the actors dressed for their parts in the film being made. The film, entitled *The Rolling Road*, was eventually shown at the *Regent* Cinema in Yarmouth.

The comings and goings of the tall ships more or less finished before the Second World War. In June 1934 the Swedish three-masted schooner *Primo* came to Great Yarmouth, then in July of that year the Danish *Frida*, August the Finn *Svenborg*, September the Swedish *Helga*, followed by *Gullkroner*, *Saturn* and *Frideborg*. In 1935 the Finn schooner *Madare* visited the town and made several repeat visits before the outbreak of war. A few sailing vessels have visited Yarmouth since the war, one being the fine Swedish *Albatross*, a four masted schooner which carried 9903 square feet of sail and unloaded a large cargo of timber at the Bollard Quay in 1955. Another relic of the 1930s period was the 'well ship', an unusual type of sailing craft for the simple reason that part of her six holds were flooded with water to accommodate conger eels. The flooded wells were necessary to keep the fish alive until the vessel reached port.

In more recent times the town was visited by the *Charlotte Rhodes*, the vessel made famous by the BBC television serial *The Onedin Line*. However members of the public who boarded her were disappointed to find the hold bare, for they had expected to see the well-furnished and upholstered interior seen on television; such scenes had of course been filmed in a studio. Another recent visitor, which unfortunately met an untimely end, was the brigantine *Luna* which, within a few days of visiting Yarmouth, was smashed to pieces on Caister beach in October 1981. Fortunately these picturesque craft have not entirely disappeared, as various countries have preserved them for posterity.

This is perhaps a romantic view of maritime Yarmouth. Today the port still flourishes. Huge container ships can be seen coming up the river to the Norfolk Line depot. Tugs and other vessels supporting the oil and gas industry line the wharfs where once herring drifters were moored and shipbuilding and repairing continues. But this is *Great Yarmouth Remembered* and I like to remember forests of masts, paddle tugs, steam and sail!

▲Yarmouth Beachmen 1908.

◄ Two old and popular Port tugs, the *Tactful*, in front, and the *George Jewson* towing a timber ship into harbour in 1927.

▲ A stately ship of the past — the Finnish barque *Lingard* awaiting ballast before putting out from the port. In the foreground is a humble shrimp boat and on the left *HMS Fitzroy,* a survey vessel.

◄ A picturesque collier-brigantine being towed into port by the *Fastnet* which was the first screw driven tug to work at the port.

◀ If the skipper of a present day ship went to sea wearing a bowler hat there would no doubt be howls of derision. Not so in Edwardian days! The piece of machinery in the foreground is the vessel's bilge pump — it must have been a back breaking job to operate, and uncomfortable too, in stormy weather.

The ship is moored at South Quay — note the trees in the background, sadly long gone.

▲ However many different types of ship must the Port of Yarmouth have seen? This is a 'Turret' ship in port in 1912.

◀ The barque *Fred* bringing in cargo of timber from the Baltic in 1926. The windmill, aft, was used to drive the bilge pumps.

▲ Now no longer with us — the old Gorleston Pier Lighthouse and curious signalling system. The lighthouse keeper, Mr. R. C. Soames, has just removed a third pennant and is about to re-hoist the signal indicating that the water at Yarmouth bar has dropped a foot.

Fishing

For hundreds of years Great Yarmouth has been famed for its herring, and as already mentioned in another chapter, owes its very existence to that luscious delicacy. At one time most of the local vessels were 'luggers', so called because they had three irregular square or lug sails, and were noted for their swiftness, but eventually steam became the driving force. At first very unpopular because of frequent breakdowns, in time the steam vessels, with their more powerful engines, fished alongside the sailing craft, and gradually replaced them. Later still came the introduction of the internal combustion engine as a means of propulsion for the fishing fleet and this, in turn, although unpopular at first because it was thought the catch of herrings would smell and taste of oil fuel, became an accepted part of the fishing fleet, and the 'steamer' a rarity.

No sooner did the holiday-maker bid farewell, at the end of each summer, to the sunny beaches of Yarmouth, than another influx of visitors arrived, but this time from the sea. First one, then another Scottish herring drifter would push their squat bows through the seas to the harbour and the river Yare. Crowds would line the piers to watch the skippers easing their craft to the quayside with hardly a bump. Then by train came the gutting and packing girls from faraway Banff, Buckie, Stornaway and other outposts of Scotland. They arrived in long shawls and longer skirts, and made for their digs, which were boarding houses which had been stripped to the bare boards, with just a white deal table at which to eat their meals. For chairs they used their trunks, which carried spare clothing and, most importantly, their oil skins. What with the smell of fish from their unenviable jobs, plus the fact that quite a number of them came from a peat burning community, the smell of the room was far from sweet.

Probably the most lucrative seasons were those immediately prior to World War I, with 1913 the most prosperous ever. In that year 835 million herrings, weighing some 157,000 tons, were landed by 1,163 vessels. What a sight it was to see them queuing up at the entrance to the harbour, awaiting their turn to pass up the river to the fish wharf. Smoke belched from their funnels making the sky around them go dark. And . . . what a scene there was on the fishwharf itself. To the casual observer — and there were many who came from miles away just to witness the wonderful sight — everything seemed to be utter confusion. Vessels in their scores were continually arriving with fish, and departing again for the fishing grounds, giving strident blasts on their sirens, or piercing shrieks with their whistles. The auctioneer would ring his bell for another 'sale'. Horses, waiting with their carts containing empty swills to hold the freshly caught fish, would neigh and klaxon and motor horns vie with each other to make the most noise. In addition, the noise of the heavy sea boots worn by both men and girls, and the iron bound wheels of the laden carts as they went over the cobbled surface of the wharf would add to the din. The exhaust steam of the windlass, the shouting of the crews to those ashore, and not least the ear-piercing shrieks of hundreds of sea gulls perched on roofs or swooping to snatch a nice fat herring from the hold — all these combined to give a good impression of 'bedlam'.

What an unforgettable sight it was to see the Scots fisher girls gutting the herrings, with a dexterity and quickness which deceived the eye. All their fingers were bandaged to prevent them getting cut, and they worked at troughs containing the fish, dressed in their oil skins. The girls — they were all called 'girls' irrespective of age — were a sturdy race, as indeed they had to be, standing for hours on bitterly cold days, in rain, hail and snow, handling the ice-cold fish and packing them with alternate layers of salt into thousands of barrels destined for the Low Countries and Russia. Thousands upon thousands of barrels could be seen and it seemed incredible that enough fish could be caught to fill them. Sometimes, in an 'off' period, the lasses had nothing to do, so they reverted to knitting or indulged in impromptu dancing, or just listened to one of the 'Hot Gospellers' that abounded there at that time of year.

If one could summon up enough courage to take a trip with the fleet to Smith's Knoll, the fishing ground, it was a very worthwhile experience and one not easily forgotten. The drifters put out to sea towards evening, for most of the fishing was done at night, and the nets were paid out. Most vessels carried over a mile of nets and these were suspended in the water from corks or bladders and hung like a curtain in the sea. Fish swimming near the surface got their gills enmeshed in the nets and, unable to escape, were hauled aboard and down into the holds, a glittering heavy mass of silver. It was no small task hauling these laden nets on board, especially in the teeth of a gale and bitterly cold weather. When sufficient fish had been caught, the skipper turned his vessel to port and with all possible speed hastened to get the best price for his catch on the market. His colleagues did likewise, and the air was often black with the smoke given off by coaling up the furnaces in the mad race to port. Some craft were so deeply laden that the sea broke over the sides.

Very often on a visit to the wharf, it was quite possible to get a string of twenty herrings for a nominal 'tanner' (an old sixpence). When reading about the enormous catches of herring, one is often confused by the words 'warp', 'cran', 'last' and even 'hundred'. The 1357 Statute of Herring fixed the method of counting and ruled that there were to be four herring to a 'warp', counted by picking up two fish in each hand. There were to be six score, that is one hundred and twenty to the 'hundred', and ten 'hundreds' to the 'cran'. In other words, 1200 fish, or ten 'crans', to the 'last', which would be roughly two tons in weight. Later on, owing to the fish diminishing in size, the 'long hundred' became 132 instead of 120. Usually the measurement was 'crans' that the boats brought in, and 'lasts' that were bought.

When the author was a youngster, the night scene at the wharf would outdo many summer seaside illuminations for the whole place would be a blaze of light. Kerosene lamps would be hissing and fluttering from the post holding the troughs, there would be flares shooting up from cotton waste floating in oil drums, more flares on the boats, and in the fishwharf buildings, mast headlights, port and starboard (red and green) on the drifters and candle lamps on the horse carts. As in the daytime, pandemonium reigned. Any fish that slipped off the baskets as they were winched ashore would be pounced upon by urchins risking their necks or a kick from behind, and everywhere there was a smell of wood burning, from the numerous smoke-houses which 'cured' the herrings.

The fishermen and packing girls alike were deeply religious. The menfolk never went to sea to fish on the Sabbath and on that day, the river was a picture, so packed with craft that it is said that one could easily clamber from vessel to vessel, from one bank to the other. At the close of the fishing season, a 'Festival of the Seas' service was held and many churches and chapels were filled almost to overflowing. The pulpit would be decorated as a wheelhouse, complete with lifebelts and port and starboard lights to throw their colours on the congregation. Nets hung from the gallery festooned down to the aisles with silver 'fish' entwined in the mesh, and bladders normally used for suspending the nets in the sea were dotted about the choir seats. While the sermon was preached, the main chapel lights were extinguished leaving only the preacher's lamp and the port and starboard lights glowing in the gloom. All this combined with the eloquence of the preacher and his hell-fire theme made a very inspiring and unforgettable scene. After the service, the men would congregate in groups, waiting to meet their 'chummies' or the lasses. A favourite haunt was King Street, but most locals avoided the Jetty Road corner, named by them 'Spit Head' through the Scots habit of chewing hard twist tobacco, and then spitting it out!

Towards late November the catches diminished and the boats prepared to go home. The girls returned to their families by train, and the boats put out to sea, laden this time not with fish but with furniture, goods and Christmas presents, bought in the town, for their families. Sadly this no longer happens for this one-time big industry has now finished. Just twenty-five to thirty years ago, herring were so plentiful that a factory was designed and built at Yarmouth at a cost of £100,000 to refine the surplus herring into oil. Thousands upon thousands of herring were all piled up by a bulldozer, ready to turn the huge mass into oil. The Herring Reduction Factory was the first of its kind in the United Kingdom, and was equipped to process seven to eight hundred cran of herring a day. Now the factory has gone, as have the girls, the sailing smacks, the Fifties and Zulus, the steam drifter with its cute red mizzen sail, and the wharf's offices have been pulled down. The old gas and oil lamps have gone, as have the naphtha ones which were once used when transferring the herrings from the boats to the wharf at night. The Scots fishing crews no longer wear their braces outside their guernseys, but dress like the 'average' man. The fishing stage curtain has come down, and the whole scene faded away except in people's memories and fortunately on photographs, taken by keen photographers who had the foresight to record an era of Yarmouth's maritime history.

There are two momentous occasions concerning the fishing industry that Yarmouthians will never forget, however, and both happened on Trafalgar Day. The first was on 21st October 1930 when the Prince of Wales, later to reign briefly as King Edward VIII, came to the fishing fleet, and boarded a herring drifter returning to port with a load of fish. He also visited some of the numerous fish curing houses, before performing the important task of officially opening the newly-built Haven Bridge which had cost £200,000 to construct.

The second memorable occasion was on the Trafalgar Day of 1957, when English and Scots drifters briefly broke off from their autumn fishing to take part in the first review of the herring fleet off Yarmouth. It was the first, and the last, for the North Sea shoals of herring were already dwindling, mainly because of gross overfishing through the years by foreign boats, who had been trawling up immature fish with close-mesh nets, preventing the small young fish from getting away to breed. Drifters decorated with flags and bunting sailed in one long seven mile line, past *H.M.S. Wave*, the leader of the Royal Navy's Protection and Minesweeping Squadron, anchored off the Britannia Pier along with other naval vessels. Admiral Sir Frederick Parham took the salute from his vessel as 170 fishing vessels passed by, making for the fishing grounds. The unusual procession was watched by thousands of spectators who had gathered at the water's edge and on the pier. At Yarmouth's South Quay a banquet was held, the chief guest being the Minister of Agriculture, Fisheries and Food, Mr. Derek Heathcote Amory, who said that "although the herring fishery was going through a most difficult time, it had seen dark days on other occasions, and light would surely come again this time". And sure enough, in 1984, the ban on herring fishing was lifted and a new landing quay made at Gorleston for the benefit of inshore fishermen in the hope that this once flourishing industry may see a revival. There has even been an advertising campaign on television to persuade more people to eat herrings — based on the Robinson Crusoe and Man Friday theme — seeking to convey the fact that "Herring are good for you". Let us hope that this age-old industry for which Yarmouth has long been famed may know an unparallelled revival for many years to come.

No Scots fisherman would put to ▶ sea on a Sunday. This photo taken, in 1926, shows the Scottish drifters in harbour — moored both sides of the river — observing the Sabbath rest.

▲Taken in 1908, one of the old steam and sailing drifters passing the 'Dutch' pier at Gorleston on its way to the fishing grounds. Note the 'Woodbine' funnel.

Steam drifters at Yarmouth 1945.▶

◄Scots fisher girls — they were always called girls irrespective of age — in 1924. They were paid £2 each per week plus 2/6d to a team of 3 girls for each barrel filled.

▲On the Fish Wharf in 1926. A horse and cart loaded with 'swills' for the herring. Yarmouth and Lowestoft were the only ports in the country where this type of basket was used.

◄Fishwharf at Yarmouth at the beginning of the century, the herring catch being unloaded. The record season was 1913 when an estimated 835 million fish were landed and sold for about £1,000,000. Note the masts of the windjammer at the top right of the photograph.

▲Archer's Curing Yard with fisher folk dressed in 'oilies'. About 1914.

▼In 1954 too many fish were caught and these 'silver darlings' are ready for the herring reduction factory which had been built on the South Denes to turn the surplus herring into meal and oil.

▲ Towards the end of an era? The Fishing Fleet Review, October 21st (Trafalgar Day) 1957. 152 English and Scots fishing craft in a line stretching for 7½ miles passed a 'saluting base' opposite the Britannia Pier.

▼ But hope for the future! The new quay built at Gorleston for inshore craft now that the ban on herring fishing has been lifted.

▲All that remained of Nelson's Jetty after the surge.

The 1953 Floods

1984 saw the thirty-first anniversary of the East Coast Floods, for on 31st January 1953 tempestuous seas wrought havoc and destruction all along the coast from Lincolnshire to Canvey Island. Many lives were lost, farmland was submerged, thousands of houses and shops were flooded, seaside piers and promenades smashed to pieces, rivers polluted, drains and sewers put out of action and quite large ships were actually lifted from their moorings to crash on hard concrete quays. Without any warning, water came rushing into people's homes, forcing them to retreat to upstairs rooms, and even onto roofs in some cases. Furniture floated about in the rooms, some houses collapsed, farmyard animals were drowned and many people had to be rescued by boats, Nelson's famous jetty was almost reduced to rubble. Concrete blocks on the parade were lifted up and tossed about like corks and the swimming pool was half-wrecked, as were the bowling greens on the Marine Parade. The solid concrete shelters near the Nelson Gardens were ripped to pieces, the Marina was inundated and iron and concrete seats on the Parade became just grotesque shapes. The Fish Wharf was flooded, as were Southtown Road and parts of Gorleston. The new road from Acle to Yarmouth was impassable owing to the flooding and breaching of Breydon. Once golden sands now became just mud and filth, having been thrown up by the sea as if a giant plough had run amok.

It was the worst flooding in British history. In Great Yarmouth alone, nine people died and ten thousand houses were affected by the floods. Unlike many other places, Yarmouth was hit from the front and the rear. The sea swept over the sandy beaches and the sea wall and waves crashed against the doors and windows of holiday hotels. Not far away, the river Bure overflowed its banks, and the walls of Breydon were breached. Those who had sought safety in the Southtown area from the invasion of the sea were trapped in the new flood waters that came in from Breydon and the marshes. Gorlestonians who had experienced gales and flooding before went to pubs and dances as usual that night, but were jolted out of their complacency when quite suddenly the bars of quayside pubs became waist deep in water. The coast watcher in the lantern house at the end of Gorleston Pier had a terrifying experience as sea and river became one; the pier itself swayed under his feet and the lantern house was pounded by the waves. Isolated too was the coastguard station, situated halfway along the pier.

But it was not enough to escape the fury of the ocean — people had to be rescued. Small boats from the seafront waterways were amongst those which sailed the streets, rescuing people from their flooded homes. One couple sat through the dark hours with their cat and dog on a table as the water rose around them. Volunteers came forward to plunge through the icy water looking for people who might be in trouble. The George Medal was given to leading fireman Fred Sadd who, throughout the night, went from house to house, swimming when necessary, guiding boats to people needing to be rescued. At Cobholm a family spent the night on their bungalow roof surrounded by water.

When the night of terror was over, and the sea returned to normal, the massive job of clearing up began. Mud and slime were everywhere. Wood blocks from the South Quay were gathered by householders as fuel for drying out their houses. Food and clothing were distributed, rest centres opened and schools and holiday camps used to house the homeless. Service men came to help civilians who were working day and night, under the beam of searchlights, to plug the broken bank of Breydon, and the adjacent embankment. In Yarmouth alone, 3500 homes were flooded, 1200 were left in need of repair, 4675 buildings lost their electricity supply and 4610 claims were made for flood relief, while it was estimated by a mathematician that 388 million gallons of flood water had poured in upon the town! It was a night that will never be forgotten by any Yarmouthian who lived through it, for it was the night the sea went mad.

◄The aftermath of the floods in 1953. Already most of the debris has been cleared up and here part of the promenade, between Wellington Pier and the Jetty is being put in order ready for the summer visitors.

▲ Near the harbour mouth — concrete slabs ripped up, seats demolished, iron railings bent.

▼ The R.A.F. came to help the distressed people of the town by providing machines, normally used for warming-up aeroplane engines during cold weather, to dry out flooded homes.

Lifeboats, Wrecks and Lifesaving

Great Yarmouth is well-steeped in lifeboat and lifesaving history. In 1849 a Yarmouth man, James Beeching, won a hundred guinea award for designing the first self-righting lifeboat, designed on the lines of the famous Yarmouth yawls which his firm used to build. Caister held the record for saving more lives than any other lifeboat station in the British Isles, but personal achievements deserve a mention too. Gorleston's 'grand old man' William Fleming was credited with helping to save 1188 lives from shipwreck, and a Captain Manby, a barrack master of Yarmouth, invented the line-throwing gun which has since been modified and has been the means of saving thousands of lives at sea.

The golden sands seen by the summer visitor to Yarmouth have been the scene of many shipwrecks and temporary strandings, making them anything but golden to the unfortunate seamen and owners of ships that run into trouble there. Before the advent of the Royal National Lifeboat Institution and lifeboats as we know them today, the saving of lives and ships at sea was left to fast-sailing yawls and luggers. These were worked and owned by private companies which allotted shares to the crews, and divided amongst its members all the money earned on salvage. They were not paid for saving life, but later they banded together and called themselves the "Norfolk Association for Saving Life from Shipwreck". Thus the Great Yarmouth lifeboat station was established by this Association, and was subsequently brought under the management of the R.N.L.I. in 1857. Yarmouth had two lifeboat stations and there were four more at Gorleston, the latter having had *six* lifeboats at one time!

It was said that four-fifths of the ships lost off the British Isles occurred off the coasts off Norfolk and Suffolk. The Caister station, whose contribution to lifesaving was 1814 lives, unfortunately lost some of her own men when their lifeboat *Beauchamp* capsized in the surf, drowning nine of her crew. Yarmouth's station was located centrally on the Marine Parade and housed three lifeboats, the *John Burch*, the surf boat *Duff* (later renamed *Abraham Thomas*) and the *Hugh Taylor*. Many years ago the youngsters took great delight in clambering over them in the shed, or watching their performance as they were pulled to the beach for launching, the huge caterpillar wheels of the carriage churning up the sand. At the actual launching into a rough sea, men went into the water up to their waists, pushing and shoving with poles to get the boat under way, and then hoisting the sails when the oars had been shipped, before the wave-tossed voyage to the distressed vessel.

The Yarmouth station was closed in 1919, when Gorleston boats assumed all responsibility. Up to that time, regattas were held off Yarmouth, which brought neighbouring lifeboats to the scene, while local fishing boats had races between them. Flags were flown and huge crowds gathered on the beach to watch the proceedings. When the lifeboats were on the shore, onlookers who peered over the side often wondered why the boats had so many bags of stones or shingle strewn about the floorboards. This acted as ballast so that when the vessel heeled over in the wind, the crew could throw the bags to the opposite side to counter the luff of the vessel.

When the Yarmouth station closed, Gorleston assumed much of the responsibility for saving life in that area. The *Elizabeth Simpson* was probably Gorleston's most famous volunteer lifeboat. Manned by a beach company, she served from 1888 until 1939 and during that fifty-one years service, she never capsized, never lost any of her crew and never lost a 'guest'. She was built at Yarmouth by James Beeching and her cost, including all gear, sails and oars was £300. Today lifeboats cost up to £400,000 to build and fit out.

Sailing ships by the score have foundered and been wrecked off Yarmouth and Gorleston, and plenty have been washed ashore. Stately windjammers, schooners, brigs, brigantines, sailing and steam fishing boats, oil tankers, timber ships and even warships have been ensnared by the dangerous sands, and certain cargoes have always increased the risk of a shipboard fire. On one memorable occasion in December 1927, a large cargo vessel laden with timber from the Baltic ports, the *Oscar*, caught fire and burned fiercely for four days and nights. Her deck cargo of timber was washed overboard and deposited in huge heaps on the sands which from the shore looked like nests built by giant pre-historic birds. Another vessel, the *Porthcawl*, which caught fire on 14th September 1933, was laden with esparto grass. Crowds of people lined Yarmouth's promenade to watch and like the *Oscar* before her, she burned for four days and nights until her burnt out hull was beached.

The year 1927 saw quite a number of wrecks on Yarmouth's shore. In December a sailing ketch, the *Sussex Belle*, dragged her anchors and came ashore at the harbour's mouth. Her captain and crew took to the rigging but their shouts for help were not heard owing to the roaring surf and howling wind. Eventually during a lull in the storm, their shouts were heard and a rescue was made by breeches buoy, but the vessel remained to be battered by the waves. On 21st November of that year the Lowestoft sailing smack, the *Lily of Devon*, grounded on the beach at Lowestoft after missing the harbour entrance. She remained there for many years, a hazard to fishermen and bathers alike, until she was blown up a few years later. Also in November 1927, the Dutch tanker *Georgia* ran aground on the Happisburgh Sands and eventually broke in two, one part drifting away with sixteen men on board, and the other half remaining aground with the Captain and fourteen crew. The Gorleston, Cromer and Southwold lifeboats went to her aid and all the men were saved.

On 9th February 1929, the sailing barge *Britannia* came ashore at Yarmouth after her crew had been saved by the rocket brigade at Gorleston; in no time at all she was battered to pieces. Just a few months later, another barge, the *Scotia*, ran ashore at almost the same spot as the *Britannia*; her sails were blown to ribbons and debris dashed against her hull until eventually time and tide broke her up. Two months later the steam fishing drifter *Tryphena* broke away from a tow into harbour because of engine trouble and she was carried by the force of the tide round the pier and on to the beach where she eventually broke up. In February 1932, the steamship *Castle Galleon* was driven ashore at Hemsby. Her crew were saved by the Winterton Rocket Brigade and taken to the Sailors' Home at Yarmouth. On 2nd April of that year she was freed from the sand and returned to active service. Two months later, the same steamship was in a collision at sea and the Gorleston lifeboat put out to rescue the crews. The rescued crewmen were again taken to the Sailors' Home where they were greeted as old friends! The last rescue made by the official lifeboat, the *Jose Neville*, was for the Lowestoft trawler *Loch Lorgan* in December 1963. The trawler stranded on the dreaded Scroby Sands and her crew of seven were taken off by the Caister men. Great seas were sweeping over the stricken vessel when she was suddenly lifted and washed ashore on Yarmouth sands. There she remained for many days, but she was eventually towed off, repaired and able to join the fishing fleet again.

Probably the worst shipping disaster, in terms of damage to the seas, shoreline and wildlife living on them, occurred in May 1978 when the Greek oil tanker *Eleni V* was rammed by a French bulk ore carrier and cut clean in two six miles off Winterton. Thick black oil from the tanker was soon polluting the sea and beaches for more than twenty miles. A fleet of ships was engaged to fight the oil menace with sprays and as the formerly golden beaches were slowly restored to their former state, the *Eleni V* was towed far out to sea where one massive explosion consigned her to a watery grave.

'Lifeboat Day' during Regatta Week 1909. The lifeboat *Hugh Taylor* is being exhibited on the ▶ beach in an interesting period photograph. The small round building on the left is the *Camera Obscura*.

▲The old Lifeboat shed with the lifeboats *John Burch* and *Duff* in 1903. The station was closed in 1919 when the Gorleston station assumed all responsibility for this part of the coast. Note the observation tower on the left from which a lookout would be kept for ships in trouble or needing a tow or food and water.

◄ The Gorleston Lifeboat, *Elizabeth Simpson*, built on the lines of the famous yawls by Beeching of Yarmouth. She served from 1888 till 1939, saved over 500 lives, never capsized and never lost a member of her crew or a 'guest'.

▲ Yarmouth's last lifeboat *The Hugh Taylor*. The craft was towed to the water on its carriage by horse. The large crew was necessary as this was a 'pulling and sailing' vessel.

◄ The Gorleston Lifeboat *John and Mary Meiklam* encountering rough water at the harbour bar as she returned from rescuing six mariners from the steamer *Fox*.

◀ In December 1963 the Lowestoft trawler *Loch Lorgan* became stuck on the Scroby sandbank. Then the rising tide lifted her off and washed her ashore on Yarmouth beach. The crew were rescued by the Caister lifeboat *Jose Neville*, on what was to be her last service.

▲ In May 1978 the Greek oil tanker *Eleni V* was cut in two by a French ore-carrier. The result was horrendous, with crude oil washing up on to the beach, causing great concern to the holiday industry and bird lovers in particular.

In the background is the remains of the wreck of the *Polaris* which came to grief in 1973.

◀ A fire broke out on the timber carrier, the *Oscar*, on 19th December 1927 and the vessel then burned for four days. Much of the cargo was washed up on the shore in heaps looking like the nests of a flock of giant prehistoric birds.

The Changing Face of the South Denes

The South Denes at Yarmouth — once just waste ground; today, worth millions of pounds. Since earliest times, the Denes were by an ancient charter to be used exclusively for drying fishermen's nets, and thus it was, until only comparatively recently. They have had an interesting and chequered history. In 1599 when a sixth haven was being built at Yarmouth, a party of rebels under Robert Kett came to the town and tried unsuccessfully to hinder the works. In both 1800 and 1801 Lord Nelson landed at Yarmouth jetty, accompanied on the first occasion by Sir William and Lady Hamilton, and walked across the Denes to the Naval Hospital to visit seamen wounded during the Battle of Copenhagen who were receiving treatment there.

Emigrants used to muster at the 'White House' on the Denes (it is now used as a store) before embarking for Canada, travelling not by some lavishly equipped ocean liner, but a small sailing 'packet' which had everything but comfort. Whale oil was stored on the Denes and as witness to the whaling industry, huge whales' jaw bones were erected and formed an archway in a road leading to Nelson's Monument.

The book *David Copperfield* also owes its inspiration to the South Denes. Charles Dickens met a native of the town — Mr. James Sharman — who inhabited a lean-to shed built of timber from wrecked ships, and it was his tales of shipwreck that started the idea for the book. It is widely believed that the actual shipwreck in the story was based on a perilous adventure of Sharman's many years before.

In stark contrast to Ham Peggotty and his exploits, the first German Zeppelin was shot down by a seaplane from the South Denes Royal Naval Air station, where huge hangars had been erected. These were later taken over by the Royal Air Force. The German Navy even bombarded Yarmouth on the 25th April 1916 in an effort to destroy this seaplane base. A submarine depot ship, the *Alecto*, was moored nearby, as was the monitor *Lord Roberts*, with its fifteen inch gun which when fired on one occasion blasted out all the windows of nearby Gorleston!

A fine racecourse used to grace the large open expanse of the Denes, bringing both gentry and commoners to the town for the meetings. Most elderly people, however, remember them best through the wonderful panorama, perhaps best represented by the Autumn fishing season when thousands upon thousands of barrels could be seen spread across the Denes, being filled with salted herrings by a host of Scots fisher lassies.

Later came Sir Alan Cobham and his flying circus who, in addition to stunt flying, took passengers on short flights over Yarmouth. His idea at the time was to make the youth of the day "conscious of air travel". Judging by today's practice of package holidays and football fans flying to distant lands for a match, he was certainly successful! Rather more down to earth, a Royal Show was once held on the Denes with all the fat cattle and sheep, show-jumping and so on connected with these events. Musical accompaniment was provided by a fine military band.

The Denes have been used as a camping ground for soldiers, cadets and boys' clubs, not to mention holiday-makers, for many years. Less conventional tourists have been known to stretch makeshift tarpaulins from their motorcycles to the ground to provide some sort of shelter and privacy, but round bell tents have been the usual form of accommodation on the South Denes.

Football matches were often played on the Denes, but in the more peaceful moments of a summer's day, in contrast to the shouts of football supporters, the shrill notes of a skylark could be heard. When, during the last war, many children were evacuated from London to Yarmouth, it became evident that such sounds were unheard of in that great metropolis. One child, hearing a skylark for the first time, ran to his teacher shouting "Here, come quick mister, there's a bloomin' sparrow got stuck up in the air, an' 'e ain't 'alf 'ollerin' "!

Predictably, the revolution or advance guard of industry finally came to the Denes, in the form of a herring reduction factory, to reduce into oil the millions of surplus herrings. By a strange quirk of fate, no sooner had the factory been built than the herring catches ceased. Consequently the factory was pulled down to make way for the huge B.P. Oil Company's storage tanks looking for all the world like a gasworks. South Denes power station was then built, taking up quite a considerable amount of space, its huge chimney of some 300 feet quite dwarfing the adjacent Nelson's Monument. Finally came the sea gas and oil boom when every piece of ground was snatched up and the Denes as some knew them were no more. Stores, yards, compounds, buildings, offices, loading bays were all erected, notices put up to keep away trespassers, and the freedom of the ancient Denes and their adjacent riverside was gone for good. Factories abound and the whole area has become heavily industrialised. Since 1964 Yarmouth has grown from nothing on the offshore oil map to one of the largest bases in Europe, with nearly a hundred firms involved. It is sad that this piece of ground across which one could once roam at will is now unavailable.

▲ South Denes power station, one of the first intruders onto the South Denes. Opened in 1958 it has four turbines and is oil fired. Its chimney which dwarfs the previous nearby landmark, the Norfolk Pillar (or Nelson's Monument, if you prefer) is 360 feet high.

▼One of the leisure activities that gained in popularity after World War Two was camping and many holiday makers were able to come to Yarmouth and erect their tents on the South Denes.

◀ The *South Gate*. It was in the year 1285 that the fortification of Yarmouth began, commencing with King Henry's Tower (named in compliment to the monarch who sanctioned the undertaking) which was 40 yards north east of St. Nicholas' Church. By slow degrees the work proceeded southwards and by 1337 work had progressed as far as *Black Friars Tower*. Then the works proceeded westwards to within a few yards of the river Yare itself. At this point, crossing the road leading from the Quay into the South Dene the *South Gate* was erected. This is reported as "Consisting of a square curtain, over an archway four yards wide, and flanked on either side by a circular embattled tower." Of this gate, a commission appointed in 1625 to survey the defences of Yarmouth reported that it was "Very fairly built with two spacious towers," adding — "It is very convenient that a 'Murdering Piece' should be planted on its Eastern Tower." The entire structure which occupied 22 yards in extent was removed in 1912.

▲ Empty barrels stacked on the South Denes ready to be filled with herrings for export to the Low Countries and Russia. Also in the photograph is what is officially known as the 'Norfolk Pillar' although why most people do not know. It is better known as 'Nelson's Monument' and was paid for by public subscription and erected in 1817. It has recently been restored and is open to the public at certain times. At 144 feet high it was not the highest point in Yarmouth although only just beaten into second place by the spire of St. Nicholas' Church which was 168 feet high. Then it was relegated to third place by the revolving tower near Britannia Pier. Both these latter are no longer with us and for a period after the War, Britannia reigned supreme atop her column. She is now, though, overlooked by the power station chimney which stands over twice as high — another 216 feet in fact.

◀Hundreds of years ago a Royal Charter was granted "that fishermen shall have the use of the South Denes, for drying their nets." This practice continued until comparatively recently when the Council sold the Denes which have been converted to industrial use.

▲This is how the South Denes looked in 1955. Can you believe it?

◀This building, known as the 'White House', still stands on the South Denes within the power station perimeter and is believed to have been built between 1780 and 1800 and is the port's last link with its seaborne trade with America. The quayside adjoining the building was known as 'American Wharf' because the vessels from Baltimore, New York and Boston, U.S.A., unloaded their cargo there between 1800 and 1830. The building has since served as a store and warehouse for the Port Authorities.

Sir Alan Cobham, who died in 1973, brought ▶
his 'Flying Circus' to Yarmouth and Gorleston
in 1929. He was a pioneer of commercial aviation and it was his desire to make the nation's
youth conscious of air travel.

▼Sir Alan Cobham's plane *Youth of Britain* in
which he gave school children flights over
Yarmouth.

River Crossings

▲ In Medieval time the authorities imposed a heavy tax on persons using the Haven bridge to the detriment of the far from well off traders who wished to take their produce and wares to Yarmouth to sell. The monks from the priory at Gorleston sought to alleviate the difficulty by operating a ferry from Gorleston and a Charter granting operational rights was granted during the reign of King John. The ferry has continued until the present day and has seen another ferry working in the South Quay area come and go. The boat shown in the photograph was formerly a lifeboat carried by the passenger liner *Esperance Bay.*

▲ The ferry early this century approaching the Gorleston side. The boats were smaller then, but solidly built, and it must have been hard work rowing back and forth. In 1939 the fare for a crossing was one halfpenny.

▲The 'old' Haven bridge. This was the sixth bridge to cross the river at about this point, the present bridge being the seventh.

◄ The Hamilton-Bailey bridge which carried the A47 over the river before the present bridge was built. In the background can be seen the suspension bridge which the 'Bailey' replaced. This bridge was itself a replacement for another bridge which collapsed when a crowd which had gathered on it rushed from one side to the other to watch a clown, in a tub drawn by a team of geese, pass down the river.

The present Bridge at Yarmouth was opened ▲▶ by the Prince of Wales (later King Edward VIII) on 21st October 1930. The machinery behind the bridge is part of the temporary lift bridge which had served whilst the old bridge was being demolished and the new bridge built. This bridge cost £200,000 to build.

Gorleston-on-Sea

For many years now, Gorleston has been recognised as the 'select suburb' of Great Yarmouth because of its peace and quietness so different from the boisterous razzamatazz of the amusement arcades and flashing lights so prevalent on the 'Golden Mile' at Yarmouth.

Gorleston was in existence long before Yarmouth came into being and an old rhyme goes

Gorleston was Gorleston ere Yarmouth began,
And will be Gorleston when Yarmouth be gone.

In fact Gorleston is thought to have been one place where the Druids celebrated their mystic rites, a tradition borne out by the fact that a circle of large stones, some almost ten feet high, stood in a field called *Stone Close* until 1788. Many discoveries of urns, coins and utensils prove that it was also occupied by the Romans, and it was even a Royal Demesne in the Confessor's time. It is interesting to note that some Augustine Friars built a monastery between Southtown and Gorleston in the late 13th century, and during the 15th century, it was renowned for its great Library. Nothing now remains of this Priory but excavations in 1975-6 uncovered the foundations of the Chapter House and finds from the site included fragments of painted glass which are now on display at the Gorleston Library.

Apart from being famous for its mackerel and herring fisheries, Gorleston was also known in the 17th and 18th centuries for its whale industry, carried out off Greenland and Iceland, and its trawl fishing industry for North Sea cod was so successful that in 1856 the fishing fleets of Barking in Essex transferred their operations to Gorleston. By 1875 there were 400 trawling smacks working for the port, and Gorleston — with Yarmouth — became the most important trawling port in the country. The largest of the trawling firms was Hewett's, whose vessels were known as the 'Hewett Fleet'. However, with growing competition from the steam trawlers of Hull and Grimsby, the Gorleston industry declined, and eventually Hewett's closed down and sold their last vessels in 1903.

Gorleston itself is about two and a half miles from Yarmouth and built on the summit of a hill which gives an excellent view of the port and harbour of Yarmouth, especially worthwhile a few years back when the wharves were a hive of industry with boats arriving and leaving, and millions of silvery herrings in basket-like containers covered the wharf during the Autumn fishing season. From Gorleston, a range of picturesque hills, once known as the 'White Cliffs', run in an unbroken line to Corton and Lowestoft. Considering the size of Gorleston in the early days, it has a remarkably large church, called St. Andrews, which measured 124 feet long and 66 feet wide, built almost entirely of flint. The church, with its high elevation, more or less overlooked the town's famous 'Dutch' pier which was originally constructed of strong oak piles and had long been a favourite rendezvous for locals and holiday-makers alike. From it, one could watch the entrance and departure of ships, or see the lifeboat launch and put out to sea on an errand of mercy. Sadly, owing to the passage of time — some 300 years or so — the old wooden structure had to be replaced by steel girders and concrete, and now far from a thing of beauty, it is 'renowned' for its bleak severity.

It may seem incredible in this day and age of electricity to learn that it was not until 1852 that Gorleston had *gas* for lighting, having until that time relied on obsolete oil lamps. A gas works was erected for the sole purpose of supplying Southtown and Gorleston with that means of good lighting, although nearby Yarmouth had long enjoyed the privilege. Close by the Gorleston gas works was a rather antiquated white house standing in front of a grove of trees which was where Oliver Cromwell's granddaughter Bridget lived after she married a Yarmouth man. She was nearly as famous as her grandfather because of her eccentric ways and mode of dress, and was often to be seen in the Yarmouth streets riding her faithful steed.

At the beginning of this century, Gorleston had a fine bandstand on the cliffs where military bands used to play popular songs and excerpts from opera until it was pulled down to make way for a swimming pool and shelters. The town also once boasted a very fine, wide stretch of sands, where holiday-makers could bask in the sun while bathers and even small children could wade out to sea on a gradually shelving foreshore in perfect safety. Hundreds of bathing huts were erected and because sand was so plentiful, it was even carted off for building purposes by tumbril and two-horse teams. During the 'twenties a large marquee was erected on a piece of green near the lighthouse, later called 'Pop's Meadow'. Here, light entertainment was provided for holiday-makers and amongst those appearing were the well-known Elsie and Doris Waters of radio fame. 'Pop', incidentally, was quite a character himself and a typical theatre showman. The man who popularised flying and proved the feasibility of air trvel, Sir Alan Cobham, paid a visit to Gorleston in 1929 with his 'Flying Circus', and I was able to get him to pose for me with his plane and talk about the future of air travel. His aim was to make the "youth of England" air-conscious and this he certainly accomplished, as we can see if we consider the number of flights to the four corners of the globe each year.

The population of Gorleston has continued to expand so that today it is larger than Yarmouth's. Yarmouth, of course, built as it is on a sandbank, cannot expand and many people who work there live in Gorleston. It is probably fair to say that in some respects Gorleston has become Yarmouth's dormitory. The holiday industry has declined generally throughout the country and Gorleston has not been immune to the trend. The same has happened to the fishing industry. However one service that continues to be available to fishermen and holiday-maker alike, if they need it — and everyone hopes they do not — is that of the Gorleston Lifeboat. The R.N.L.I. station was established in 1866 and from 1883 to date has been responsible for saving 1283 lives. The most famous of the boats are the *Elizabeth Simpson* which saved 441 lives during her service and the *Louise Stephens* which took up station in 1939. She was a new type of lifeboat built at Cowes, on the Isle of Wight, and known, appropriately, as the 'Gorleston Type'. She is still in existence today, working as a pleasure boat. The most famous of the coxwains was undoubtedly William Fleming, a popular figure in the town. He helped save 1188 lives and was much decorated, having been awarded the R.N.L.I. Gold, Silver and Bronze Medals, the O.B.E. and the George Cross, in addition to a silver watch (which he *always* carried) given by Queen Wilhelmina of the Netherlands, for his fearless seamanship in going to the rescue of the Dutch steamer *Georgia*. He died in 1953.

Gorleston has never sought to attract visitors in the same way as its neighbour. The relaxation offered has always been of a more sedate nature — perhaps a walk along the cliff-top gardens, the land for which was purchased by the Council in 1928 for £27,000. In earlier times one could take a trip to Yarmouth on one of the six 'two-ended' steamers, mentioned elsewhere, or a trip to London on one of the famous Belle paddle-steamers. In 1899 the fare was five shillings single or seven shillings and sixpence return. Possibly you wanted to go to the cinema? The first, *Filmland*, opened in Beach Road on Boxing Night 1913 and was followed a week later by the *Coliseum*, a 964 seat theatre which was demolished in 1970 to make way for a shopping and car park development. *Filmland* became the *Palace* and was known locally as the 'kosey'. It had a chequered history, including a number of name changes. It was damaged during the second world war and later demolished.

Nearer the sea front the *Pavillion* was built just after the turn of the century on the hump that had been built to stop the river flowing south and gardens were laid out with a bandstand. The swimming pool was built on the site of the bandstand in 1938 together with the concert hall. Between 1919 and 1934 — a record for the East Coast — Henry Clay provided an entertainment known as *Pop's Concert Party* on 'Pop's Meadow'. Mr. Clay was a baritone who was assisted by his wife, a violinist, who also played a saw!

The building of the new pier at the river mouth was not a boon to those seeking quiet relaxation. The new pier caused the sea to come right up to the sea wall, so for part of the day Gorleston lost its lovely beach with its stalls and beach huts. It also lost the 'cosies'. These were niches in the old 'Dutch' pier in which people could sit and fish or watch the boats or just sit. The old pier with its capstans, once used to warp sailing boats into the harbour entrance, was a popular place for people to stroll, to watch the fishing boats or perhaps the launch of the lifeboat. Today, this amenity, which it must be admitted was not built with that purpose in mind, is no more. Still, Gorleston is a nice place — a place, perhaps, to escape for a little peace!

▲Gorleston at the beginning of the century. The bandstand stands on the site of the present swimming pool. Note the bathing machines and the horse which moved them tethered nearby.

▼In 1954 Gorleston still had one of the finest beaches in the country.

Gorleston 1900. The Promenade, Pier, and Cliff Hotel which was burned down. The bandstand▶ has now gone and the swimming pool stands on the site.

▲ Gorleston beach photographed on a pleasant August evening in 1984 — and almost deserted. The photo shows how the rebuilt pier has affected the beach. All the huts have gone because the sea now comes to the sea wall and yacht pond.

◄The old 'Dutch' Pier with holidaymakers settled comfortably into the 'cosies'.

▲The 'Old' Coastguard station on Gorleston Pier. A 'South cone' has been hoisted — this indicates that a gale is expected from the South. If the cone had been hoisted the other way up it would indicate that the gale would be expected from the North.

◄The old capstan on the Dutch Pier at Gorleston and said to date back to the reign of Elizabeth I. It is now preserved in the custody of the Yarmouth Maritime Museum.

▲ "A wonderful old man, William" they used to say in Gorleston of lifeboat coxswain William Fleming who in 48 years service with the Royal National Lifeboat Institution helped to save 1188 lives. He was a cabin boy on a fishing boat at 12, a lifeboatman at 19 and died in 1954 at the good old age of 84. He was awarded the R.N.L.I. Gold Medal in 1922, the Bronze Medal in 1925 and the Silver Medal in 1927. In 1924 he was awarded the O.B.E. and in 1941 the George Medal. The award, however, that he seemed most pleased with was the gift of a handsome watch from Queen Wilhelmina of the Netherlands in recognition of his fearless seamanship displayed in the rescue of the crew of the Dutch steamer *Georgia* in 1927. After he retired as a lifeboatman he became a popular figure on Gorleston beach, taking holidaymakers for trips in his rowing boat.

Multum in Parvo

Reminiscences about old times usually bring to mind a thousand and one minor instances which may not be of sufficient import to merit a chapter of their own, but nevertheless are still part of Yarmouth's history and therefore should be mentioned. Amongst my early memories was a visit to Great Yarmouth by the 'Dough Boys'. They were part of the American Army and they sported Norfolk-type button-to-throat tunics, Khaki trousers with puttees (that is, long strips of cloth wound spirally round the leg) and boy scout hats. They came to take part in a baseball match on the Wellesley Recreation Ground. The game itself was something of an enigma to many of the locals, most of whom had never heard of the American ball game. And what a contrast their old fashioned uniforms were to the smart dress worn by American airmen during the Second World War. The boy scouts, of which I was one, were allowed to go and watch them. All seemed to be six feet tall or more, and as today, they were very friendly. After the match was over, they left the town and no more was ever heard of them.

At about the same time, and during the busy summer season, an aeroplane crashed on to Yarmouth beach near the Revolving Tower. A monoplane, it was not unlike Bleriot's famous plane, and in no time at all, souvenir hunters began tearing or cutting off pieces of the canvas wings and taking part of the fuselage, until only a skeleton remained. When summer was over and darkness fell earlier, many youngsters found it fascinating to watch the street lamplighter going round with his long pole to turn on the gas in the lamps with a resounding 'plop'. Almost up to the Second World War, it was quite usual to see a team of horses and tumbrils carting away sand from the beaches of Yarmouth and Gorleston — Gorleston would now like some of it back! How those poor beasts heaved and strained in their harnesses as they pulled heavily laden carts, the wheels of which were for ever sinking into the soft sand. Mentioning sand reminds me of the almost forgotten narrow gauge railway on the South Denes by which small wagons used to take sand to sailing ships moored at the 'dolphin'. The sand was needed for ballast to enable the ships to sail in safety after discharging their heavy cargoes of timber or whatever. Without the ballast they could easily overturn.

As schoolboys, some pals and I were very excited to hear that a tank similar to those used at Ypres and the Somme would be coming to Yarmouth, and more excited still when we were given time off to witness the event. Then we saw it, emerging from the Southtown Railway Station and cutting out huge portions of the roadway with its caterpillar tracks as it proceeded along the road to the Town Hall where it was proudly exhibited for a short time.

In the early 1900s, Yarmouth's first cinema, the *Gem* (now the *Windmill)* was opened. Some years later I saw a film there about pirates, with all the trimmings of cut-throats, daggers and cutlasses, and evil-looking men with beards and eye patches. During the film they were seen beaching a boat on a 'desert island' and then crawling with daggers in their mouths through long grass and foliage. To our amusement, we suddenly recognized our favourite haunts of Ormesby Broad and the wooden boathouse from which we hired boats — what a let-down! At the beginning of the century when there were no televisions, radios, gramophones or discos, one had to get one's entertainment in other ways. Violent storms often brought Yarmouth people out, either to see a lifeboat launched or just to watch lightning playing zig-zag on the lofty structure of the Revolving Tower. In late summer, many visitors were interested to watch the many fishing boats sailing back and forth from the Scroby Sands in what appeared to be rather an erratic manner. They would almost come ashore, then turn round and make for the Scroby sandbank again, before turning again for shore. Actually the vessel was tacking in an attempt to reach port against the wind. Another event which brought the crowds out was a 'searchlight tattoo' given by naval ships anchored in the Roads, their powerful beams lighting up many familiar places and faces.

In the 1930s, three animal characters beloved by children were *Pip, Squeak* and *Wilfred*, known to many from the pages of the *Daily Mirror*. One year the publishers

109

decided that a seaside tour by these lovable animals would not come amiss so that children could see the pets in real life. In due course 'Uncle Dick' brought the small menagerie of dog, penguin and rabbit to Yarmouth where they made their temporary home on the forecourt of the *Royal Aquarium*. Needless to say, their appearance was a great success although some of the younger children complained that the pets would not talk to them (as they did in the paper). There was further excitement when *Squeak*, the penguin, managed to escape and made straight for the Floral Gardens and the sea! After many attempts to catch her, they at last succeeded and she was put back into her cage, to the great relief of 'Uncle Dick' and the children. At about the same time, a team of girls from the *Mirror* called the '*Daily Mirror* Eight' also made a tour of the various seaside resorts, playing ball games with the summer visitors. They travelled in a luxurious streamlined van and gave their show in the Wellington Gardens. The girls were very smart and neatly dressed and gave much pleasure to those both participating in and watching the games.

To see Yarmouth's South Quay today, with its rows of parked cars, it seems incredible to think that only a few years ago, a steam engine used to pull well-laden trucks of coal along the Quay from Vauxhall Station to the Fish Wharf to fuel the boilers of the steam-driven fishing boats. Many people regret the demolition of the Breydon railway bridge which was used by passengers travelling from the Beach Station, across the mud flats of Breydon, to Gorleston and Lowestoft. With the sun setting and reflecting on the wet mud flats, it made a fine setting for a picture, of which both painter and photographer took advantage.

Yarmouth was frequently visited by warships which, anchored a mile or so off the Britannia Pier, were warmly welcomed by both townspeople and holiday-makers alike. However, the steam launches used to transport men ashore used to come in for criticism from the local boatmen as they were poorly handled and often collided with the pier as they attempted to land passengers on it. When *HMS Troubridge* visited the port, beach motor boats took many people out to board the vessel at its anchorage about a mile from shore. A shuttle service was established to take out and bring back visitors from the ship. As I awaited my turn to go on board, another beach boat could be seen transferring its passengers to the landing stage of the warship. Suddenly, a 'Mack Sennet' type comedy was enacted before our eyes as a young lady stepping from the boat to the landing stage got into difficulties. The current began forcing the motor boat away from the landing stage, and the further the current carried the boat, the further the young lady's legs were forced apart until she was nearly doing the splits. Of course she eventually fell into the water and although we felt sorry for her as she was pulled out like a half-drowned rat, it did seem funny too.

Another occasion I remember with pleasure was when a friend and I were invited by a beachman to take a trip on the 'briny'. We quickly said "yes" and almost before we realised it, we took over the oars and rowed the craft right out to the St. Nicholas Light-ship. We moored alongside it, clambered aboard and were shown the 'works', both in and around the lamp house, and then taken below to see some of the crew making mats and putting miniature ships into bottles. We then clambered back into the rowing boat and took to shore, paying the boatman although we had done all the work! Such a trip would no longer be possible because the St. Nicholas Lightship disappeared from use forty or more years ago.

These then are just some of the many memories of Great Yarmouth and Gorleston that I cherish. Never in the world's history have so many changes taken place in such a short period of time — one man's lifetime. I wonder what memories my grandchildren will cherish as they enter the twenty-first century and look back on the final decades of the twentieth?

Catlin's Royal Pierrots, a typical ▶ entertainment. They appeared at Yarmouth from 1912 to 1915 — in the open air by day and in the Britannia Pier Pavilion at night. In 1914 they received the £100 prize awarded by the Amalgamated Press Ltd. for the entertainment party voted the most popular in England that year.

▼The *Daily Mirror* tried to woo readers even before Mr. Maxwell took it over and started offering £1,000,000 prizes! In 1934 the means of publicity was the *Daily Mirror Eight*, a team of young ladies who gave gymnastic displays and played ball-games with the holidaymakers.

◄ After the First World War this tank, which first took action against the enemy at the Somme on 15th September 1916, was brought to Yarmouth as a memorial. Thousands of school children thronged the streets to watch the cumbersome vehicle tearing up great patches from the tarmac road with its great caterpillar tracks as it made its way to Hall Quay, to be finally manoeuvred into position on a wedge shaped concrete base.

▲ Places of detention as they used to be. The dungeons in the Tolhouse, Middlegate Street, 1908.

◄ The Cruiser *H.M.S. Norfolk* off Yarmouth in 1930 — warmly welcomed by the beachmen who were able to make a little money by taking sightseers out to her.

Pictures of Pure Nostalgia